W9-CJQ-960

CHRISTIAN
ETHICS
& U.S.
FOREIGN
POLICY

CHRISTIAN ETHICS & U.S. FOREIGN POLICY

MARK R. AMSTUTZ

Academie
Books
Grand Rapids,
Michigan
Zondervan Publishing House

CHRISTIAN ETHICS AND U.S. FOREIGN POLICY
Copyright © 1987 by Mark R. Amstutz
Grand Rapids, Michigan

ACADEMIE BOOKS
is an imprint of
Zondervan Publishing House
1415 Lake Drive, S.E.
Grand Rapids, Michigan 49506

Library of Congress Cataloging in Publication Data

Amstutz, Mark R.
  Christian ethics and U.S. foreign policy.

    Bibliography: p.
    1. United States—Foreign relations—1945—Moral and ethical as-
pects.   2. Christianity and international affairs.   I. Title.

E840.A67 1987   241'.624'0973   87–6251

ISBN   0–310–30031–2

Edited by Laura Dodge Weller

Printed in the United States of America

87 88 89 90 91 92 93 / CH / 10 9 8 7 6 5 4 3 2 1

To my mother,
Ruth Nelda Amstutz,
who taught me the importance of
Christian ethics

CONTENTS

PREFACE

This study is written with the conviction that Christians as individuals and as members of the body of Christ have a responsibility to influence international affairs in general and foreign policy in particular. If Christians are to discharge their civic and religious responsibilities competently, they need to be informed—theologically, ethically, and politically. The recent increased political participation of Fundamentalists, Evangelicals, and mainline Protestants in the public debates over American foreign policy suggests, however, that Christian activists need to carry out their political obligations with greater care and thoughtfulness. Rather than illuminating relevant moral norms to specific foreign policy problems and to helping establish a moral context for public policy debates, Christians have focused their attention on specific public policy choices. A regrettable consequence of this increased focus on policy advocacy has been a failure to influence the moral context of the public policy debates.

This book is written to encourage a more informed and circumspect Christian witness in the American foreign policy arena. It is written not for the specialist in ethics or foreign policy but for the citizen who believes that Christian norms can and should influence the development and implementation of foreign policy. I have not sought to provide answers to the complex problems confronting U.S. foreign policy. My aim, rather, is to illuminate relevant ethical principles and to provide some assessment of the possibilities and limits of individual and collective Christian action in foreign affairs.

In preparing this book, I have incurred many intellectual and personal debts. First, my understanding of the dilemma of ethics and foreign policy has been profoundly shaped by Christian authors who have analyzed this difficult and complex arena. Although not limited to them, I am especially grateful for the insights and arguments of John C. Bennett, Herbert Butterfield, Richard J. Neuhaus, Reinhold Niebuhr, and Kenneth Thompson. All of them, but especially Niebuhr, have contributed decisively to my own thinking.

Second, I want to thank the students in my class on Ethics and Foreign Policy for stimulating and challenging my moral analysis of foreign affairs and for encouraging me to speak to a wider audience.

Third, I am grateful to the Wheaton Alumni Association for providing me with a summer grant in 1982 to explore the moral implications of nuclear deterrence. This summer leave, along with the initiation of a course on ethics and foreign policy, provided the initial stimulus for this study.

Fourth, I want to thank the administration of Wheaton College for granting me a sabbatical leave during the fall 1985 semester. Without that leave this book would not have been written.

Finally, and most importantly, I want to thank my wife, Donna, and my two daughters, Anne and Caroline, for their support. Writing is a lonely enterprise. It removes the author from the many pleasures and responsibilities of family life. It is with profound gratitude that I acknowledge my family's contribution to this project.

INTRODUCTION

Every day the news media provides dramatic stories about the tensions, injustices, and disorder of world politics. Although all human beings desire to live in a peaceful and just world system, the conditions of the world are quite different. As I write this, the news media in recent weeks has illustrated the unstable and precarious world system with the following reports:

1. The five-year war between Iran and Iraq, which appears to have no end in sight, has resulted in nearly a million casualties.

2. Israeli jets recently carried out a surprise attack against the PLO headquarters in Tunisia. The action was allegedly retaliation for the murder of three Israeli civilians in Cyprus.

3. Palestinian guerrillas commandeered an Italian cruise ship in the Mediterranean Sea and temporarily held it in an effort to gain the release of fifty PLO prisoners in Israel. Subsequently, the guerrillas surrendered to Egyptian authorities and were later captured when U.S. military forces intercepted the commercial plane in which the guerrillas were departing Egypt. This action was taken by the U.S. because of the killing of one American during the hostage crisis.

4. The U.S. government announced limited economic sanctions against South Africa as an effort to pressure its government to abolish apartheid and to move toward a more participatory political system.

5. The Soviet Union has continued to demand that the United States stop its strategic weapons defense program (strategic defense initiative, or S.D.I.), while the United States has continued to call for substantial reductions in strategic nuclear missiles.

6. The U.S. government has announced that it will no longer grant the World Court in The Hague automatic jurisdiction in political cases. The action was prompted by the court's decision to hear Nicaragua's claim against the United States.

Events such as these remind us that world politics is often disorderly and unjust. But because the world is threatened by military conflicts, economic injustices, and political repression, Christians have a responsibility to promote human dignity worldwide. While there are many ways in which this can be done, this study focuses on the promotion of world justice by the state. Specifically, it is concerned with the development and implementation of a moral U.S. foreign policy—a diplomacy that promotes God's justice and righteousness and international peace. This is an enormously difficult and complex task. It is difficult because there are diverse ways of interpreting and applying the Scriptures to the temporal problems of the world, and complex because world affairs problems do not lend themselves to simple definition or solution. Christians may disagree theologically and hold different perceptions and conceptions about problems of world politics.

This book is written for two purposes: first, to call Christians to action; and second, to provide a framework for discussion and a guide to action on U.S. foreign policy issues. Historically, Evangelicals and Fundamentalists in the United States have given scant attention to politics and foreign policy. In the past these Christian movements encouraged, in different degrees, a pietistic, spiritualized faith that neglected the political affairs of the world. Thus many twentieth-century American Christians have grown up in the church believing that politics and foreign affairs are unimportant and that political and economic problems can best be addressed by focusing exclusively on the spiritual needs of individuals.

Because of the tendency to spiritualize problems, many Christians have assumed that the way to world peace and justice is through evangelism. Evangelism is, of course, a central task of the church, but the proclamation of the gospel does not automatically result in good foreign policy any more than it leads to good medical practice or sound business investment. World politics is an aspect of God's creation; and if Christians are to provide God's salt and light in world politics, they will have to be informed on the political issues they wish to address.

This study is written for Christians concerned with the development and implementation of a moral U.S. foreign policy. All believers are called to participate in God's kingdom in a variety of different vocations. Some are called to be diplomats or to work in public or private international organizations. Many are called to participate indirectly in foreign affairs through discussion and debate and through interest-group activities. A major goal of this study is to serve as a catalyst and guide to Christians involved in the foreign policy process. One of the gratifying developments of the past ten to fifteen years has been the growing number of Evangelicals concerned with public affairs. This concern needs to be translated into more effective collective action.

If Evangelicals are to influence foreign policy in the name of God, they need to have two types of knowledge or competency—spiritual and prudential. If a Christian is to speak credibly in the name of the Lord about, say, U.S. strategic nuclear policy, he or she needs to know God and be familiar with the problems of nuclear strategy. Regrettably, Christian activists in world affairs have often been more inspired by simplistic moralisms than by a careful and informed integration of biblical faith and a dispassionate analysis of particular problems of world politics. Indeed, one of the unfortunate legacies of increased participation by religious groups is that it has resulted in simplistic, single-issue political activism by persons who have used the Christian faith to defend a political ideology. Instead of faith informing public policy, Christianity has been used as a shield to justify particular national interests and ideological preferences. The results of such developments have been most unfortunate, for they have impoverished faith and discredited diplomacy. One of the purposes of this study, therefore, is to explore the role and application of Christian norms in the conduct of foreign affairs. My aim is to assess the limits and possibilities of a "Christian" foreign policy.

A major thesis of this study is that moral norms in general and Christian principles in particular can and must have a role in U.S. foreign relations. This role, while modest, will be central to the sustenance of a vigorous and humane diplomacy. This analysis is not concerned with Christian ethics per se or abstract morality; nor is it concerned solely with the problems of U.S. foreign policy. My aim, rather, is to show how a Christian vision can be brought to bear on the corrupt, sinful, and unjust problems of world affairs, and, more specifically, on the diplomacy of the United States. I do this by developing a framework of action in the first three chapters and by examining a number of key foreign policy problems in the remainder of the book. In chapter 1 we will look at the role of moral norms in the development and implementation of foreign policy; in chapter 2 we will examine some key biblical principles that can inspire and direct U.S. foreign policy. In chapters 3 through 7 we will analyze five specific problems: the justice of the current world system, nuclear peacekeeping, the promotion of human rights, economic assistance to the poor, and the role of the institutional church in foreign affairs.

Fundamentally, there are two ways Christian ethics can be applied to the conduct of U.S. diplomacy. The first, which might be called foundationalism, seeks to develop a clear conception of biblical morality and then to apply it to world politics. Its focus is on the exposition of biblical ethics and the development of a Christian vision of world order. It is secondarily concerned with application. The second approach, the one adopted here, is eclecticism. It assumes that the integration of faith and public policy involves a continuing dialectic between principles and public policy concerns, the Bible and diplomacy. Whereas foundationalism assumes that one begins with ethics and moves to public policy, the eclectic approach believes that there must be an ongoing interaction between faith and world politics, with the former informing the latter and the latter refining the former. While the eclectic approach is much less precise and tidy than foundationalism, it assures a vigorous and ongoing tension between faith and action, theory and practice. An approach that illuminates only a vision of the ideal world and not the problems of world affairs may contribute little to the improvement of the world itself. The challenge is not to uplift the vision, but to uplift world politics.

This study is written from a perspective of Christian realism. This perspective, identified with writers such as Reinhold Niebuhr, John C. Bennett, Kenneth Thompson, and George Kennan, has emphasized the totality and universality of sin but also the possibility of some social justice through modest, incremental public policies. Three important "realistic" elements undergird this study.

First, power is assumed to be a legitimate force in domestic and world politics. Just as the quest for domestic justice will involve the sovereign power of the state, the quest for international justice will depend on the collective and cooperative influence of nations. Whereas in domestic politics the authority of the state is used to make and enforce rules, in world politics it becomes the means to defend and promote the legitimate interests of states. Because the world involves some 160 sovereign states, the protection and promotion of rights often involves intense conflict which can be resolved only by resorting to military force.

Power is morally neutral. The challenge is to use it in the right way for the right purposes. What makes the development of a moral foreign policy such a difficult task is the pervasive temptation to misuse power. As Reinhold Niebuhr pointed out so eloquently in *Moral Man and Immoral Society*, the pride of nations can easily lead to hypocrisy and result in significant evil. Some Christians, especially pacifists, have suggested that Christians should avoid power politics altogether. While I am sympathetic with those who hold a different conception of Christian vocation, this study assumes that the search for world justice will of necessity require public policies based on state power. A sound, moral diplomacy lies in the management of power, not in its elimination or avoidance. The challenge to American Christians lies in helping to direct, sustain, and circumscribe the politics and military and economic power of the United States.

A second key assumption is the acceptance of the contemporary world system. Some Christians are fond of pointing out that God's world is fundamentally a single human community. But the view that God does not sanction the contemporary world order is not corroborated either by Scripture or significant moral or theological teaching. Human beings, after all, are not just members of a world community, but of a host of other more proximate communities, including nations, neighborhoods, professional associations, clubs, churches, and political parties. Through these smaller communities people serve and find meaning in life. Since there is nothing biblically inconsistent with the present world order, this study assumes that the contemporary world order is morally legitimate. There is, of course, nothing permanent about the current world system, but neither is there a compelling reason for its immediate termination. Our study therefore seeks to make the existing world order more just rather than trying to devise a radically new system of world community.

Finally, this study assumes that the United States has an important role and responsibility in promoting justice and protecting liberty. Because of its history, resources, and institutions of political economy, the United States can help promote human dignity by modeling practices and institutions associated with limited government and by protecting peoples from foreign aggression. This does not mean that the United States is morally superior to other nations or that God has chosen the American people, as he did the nation of Israel, to be special instruments of justice. Because of the universality and totality of sin, all nations are under the judgment of God; but recognition of the universality of God's judgment does not negate the legitimacy of national loyalties or the possibility of making choices among imperfect alternatives. Notwithstanding its many shortcomings, the historical record suggests that the United States has been a significant force for good in world affairs.

In conclusion, I wish to remind the reader that discussion and debate about the morality of public policies has often been a divisive force in the church. It is important to remember that people of good will often share common goals but hold different views about the means and methods by which such goals should be implemented. No individual or group should appropriate the authority of the church to defend particular foreign policies. As Christians we should strive toward unity in moral principles and goals but tolerate diversity in the development and implementation of prudential concerns. The bishops' pastoral letter on nuclear strategy provides wise counsel: "Not only conviction and commitment are needed in the church but also civility and charity." This study seeks to illuminate the foreign policy process and to inspire debate and action among Christians. Hopefully the unity of believers will be strengthened by this enterprise and will result in a stronger church and a better world.

1

MORALITY AND
FOREIGN POLICY

"Saints can be pure, but statesmen, alas, must be responsible."

Arthur Schlesinger, Jr.[1]

"Christianity and religion are indeed relevant to public and world affairs, both to assure a sense of righteousness and justice and to act as a safeguard against self pride and hypocrisy. Knowing this, those who hold to its truths can act with grace and confidence even in an uncertain and ambiguous realm."

Kenneth Thompson[2]

"The broad principles that should govern our international conduct are not obscure. They grow out of the practice of nations of the simple things Christ taught."

John Foster Dulles[3]

Before exploring the relationship of the Christian faith to U.S. foreign policy, it is important to define how moral norms relate to diplomacy. If we are to define the limits and

---

[1] Arthur Schlesinger, Jr., "The Necessary Amorality of Foreign Affairs," *Harper's Magazine*, Aug. 1971, p. 72.

[2] Kenneth Thompson, *The Moral Issue in Statecraft* (Baton Rouge: Louisiana State University Press, 1966), p. 127.

[3] John Foster Dulles, *A Righteous Faith for a Just and Durable Peace* (New York: Federal Council of Churches, 1942), p. 10.

possibilities of a "Christian" foreign policy, we need to know how unchanging, transcendent norms apply to the making and implementation of foreign policy.

To begin with, people are moral agents. Since people must choose between good and evil, they are unable to avoid morality. Indeed, all human choices—public or private—are based on ethical presuppositions. The apostle Paul points out (in Romans 1 and 2) that God has implanted in humankind a moral conscience—an inner sense of right and wrong, justice and injustice. While this moral conscience is rudimentary, it provides a foundation for moral judgment and action. The fact that people argue about the moral legitimacy of public policies and that they seek to defend and promote their interests in moral language is evidence of the existence and impact of morality in everyday life.

Foreign policy, like other aspects of life, is inescapably a moral enterprise. Since values are at the foundation of all public policy decision, the issue is not whether values will influence the conduct of foreign policy, but which values and in what ways. Foreign policy is not and cannot be value-free. International politics does not push decision and action beyond the realm of moral judgment, but rests on moral choice itself.

Robert Kennedy, in *Thirteen Days*, an account of the Cuban missile crisis, illustrates how ethical values can be applied in the making of public policies. According to him, the most important factor in defining what the U.S. response should be to the Soviet placement of intermediate missiles in Cuba was morality. He indicates that the officials involved in this crisis spent more time weighing and assessing the moral consequences of military action than on any other matter during the early stages of the crisis. According to Kennedy, the major reason the United States did not conduct an all-out military attack against Cuba was that such an action would "erode if not destroy the moral position of the United States throughout the world."[4] While moral discourse described by Kennedy does not assure ethical behavior, such discourse does qualify, reform, and direct action. As political theorist Michael Walzer has noted, moral discourse is "coercive."[5]

[4]Robert Kennedy, *Thirteen Days* (New York: Norton, 1968), p. 27.
[5]Michael Walzer, *Just and Unjust Wars* (New York: Basic Books, 1977), p. 12.

Recognizing that the development and implementation of foreign policy is a moral enterprise does not explain how morality should be applied to the conduct of foreign relations. It is one thing to admit that public choices rest on moral assumptions; it is quite another thing to develop a framework for explicitly applying ethical standards to diplomacy. If morality could be applied easily to the responsibilities and tasks of diplomats, there would be little need for this chapter. But the fact remains that the relationship of ethics to international politics, morality to diplomacy, has been a topic of much dispute and confusion. The aim of this chapter, therefore, is to identify the role of ethics in foreign policy and to illuminate some of the purposes and dangers of explicitly applying morality to diplomacy.

THE RELATIONSHIP OF ETHICS
AND FOREIGN POLICY

Idealism Versus Realism

Historically, there have been two dominant traditions of political morality—idealism and realism. Max Weber called these two approaches the "ethic of ultimate ends" and the "ethic of responsibility."[6] The former is concerned with intentions, while the later is concerned with the consequences of actions and policies. While both approaches seek peace and justice and the promotion of human dignity, they hold radically different presuppositions of human nature, the character of world politics, and political methodology.

Idealism is fundamentally a utopian conception of human nature and world affairs. It views the world as a fundamentally harmonious environment, with the diplomat's chief responsibility being to eliminate barriers that impede the good will of states and to bring reason and tact to bear on international disputes. This approach stresses the importance of moral norms in guiding and directing political action. It places much emphasis on defining what ought to be done and gives comparatively less attention to the problem of political method and strategy. The statesman who best exemplifies this tradition in recent history is Woodrow Wilson, a president who tried to create

---

[6] Max Weber, *Politics as a Vocation* (Philadelphia: Fortress, 1965), pp. 46–49.

international institutions built on the premise of "open covenants, openly arrived at."

Political realism, by contrast, is pessimistic about human nature and world politics. It views people as fundamentally acquisitive of power and influence and the world system as inherently conflictual. Hans Morgenthau, a leading disciple of this tradition, argues that because of the intractability of interpersonal and interstate problems, the quest for peace and justice must be based on actual behavior, not on abstract theories and moralistic cants. "If the desire for power cannot be abolished everywhere in the world," writes Morgenthau, "those who might be cured would simply fall victims to the power of others."[7] The quest for justice must therefore be rooted in the capabilities and drives of people and states, not in abstract morality. A key tenet of realists is their belief that foreign policy should be guided by the national interest rather than by ideology or morality. This does not mean, as some have suggested, that foreign policy should be based on pragmatism, but rather that foreign policy should be based on a careful definition of a state's interests and capabilities in the light of the moral claims of other states. A realistic moral foreign policy is thus one that defines and pursues national interests in terms of justice and power.

Neither idealism nor realism provides an adequate framework for a Christian political witness in world affairs. What is needed is a combination of both approaches. A satisfactory strategy of moral politics must include vision and transcendence, affirmed in idealism, and the calculation of interests and capabilities, emphasized by realism. A foreign policy devoid of idealism and realism will contribute little to international justice or world peace. The distinguished historian E. H. Carr has written about the importance of the synthesis of both approaches:

> . . . any sound political thought must be based on elements of both utopia and reality. Where utopianism has become a hollow and intolerable sham, which serves as a disguise for the interests of the privileged, the realist performs an indispensable service in unmasking it. But pure realism can offer nothing but a naked struggle for power which makes any kind of international society

---
[7] Hans Morgenthau, *Politics Among Nations*, 5th ed., rev. (New York: Knopf, 1978), p. 36.

impossible. Having demolished the current utopia with the weapons of realism, we still need to build a new utopia of our own, which will one day fall to the same weapons. The human will will continue to seek an escape from the logical consequences of realism in the vision of an international order which, as soon as it crystallises itself into concrete political form, becomes tainted with self-interest and hypocrisy, and must once more be attacked with the instruments of realism.[8]

In short, an effective political strategy requires both vision and calculation, idealism and realism.

The integration of morality and power is important not only because politics needs it, but also because the Christian faith requires it. The Christian religion is, of course, based on faith, but its fruit is borne out by faithful obedience to God—manifested in the redemptive witness of individuals and collectivities. Such a witness will involve proclamation of the gospel, but it will also include the reformation of the fallen and corrupt institutions and practices of society.

A Christian perspective on foreign policy, as I shall argue in the next chapter, provides both hope and caution, idealism and realism. Because sin and grace are woven into the fabric of human relationships, Christian politics must be principled and utopian, calling forth justice and peace; but it must also be realistic, taking into account the moral limitations of human nature. An effective Christian approach to foreign policy must therefore be based on a theory of international political reality that integrates both power and ethics, strategy and moral norms. The challenge is to harness power in the service of the common good.

Moral Principles and Statecraft

Foreign policy is the process by which governments promote the basic interests of states in the international political system. Since resources are limited and the interests of people unlimited, nations are in continuous competition and conflict over the world's tangible and intangible resources. An effective foreign policy involves not merely the expression of a nation's goals, but the articulation and implementation of interests in the light of other states'

---

[8]E. H. Carr, *The Twenty Years' Crisis, 1919–1939* (New York: Harper Torchbooks, 1964), p. 93.

interests and capabilities. The moral problem in U.S. foreign policy is how to aid in the development of diplomatic conduct whose aims and methods contribute to an international just peace.

This study is not concerned with the morality of private persons. Citizens, interest groups, religious associations, and even churches participate in the making of foreign policy. Their roles are vital in a democracy. But our concern here is focused on the public actions of people—on the governmental machinery charged with making and implementing foreign policy for the United States. The aim is to examine how moral norms relate to the conduct of diplomacy.

The relationship of moral norms to U.S. foreign policy is especially important, for Americans have historically sought to defend foreign policies by appealing to such moral values as peace, human dignity, and political freedom. The tendency towards moralism was especially manifest in the late nineteenth and early twentieth centuries. For example, President McKinley, argued that the taking of the Philippines was done for the moral good of indigenous peoples, while Woodrow Wilson believed that the U.S. intervention in Veracruz in 1914 was for the benefit of the Mexican people. More recently, President Carter gave expression to the universalistic and moralistic motif in his human rights policy—a diplomacy based on the conviction that it is the United States' responsibility to defend basic rights everywhere.

The broad shifts in U.S. foreign policy between moralism and pragmatism have generated confusion about the interrelationship of ethics and diplomacy and cast doubt on the role of transcendent norms. Arthur Schlesinger, Jr., for example, writes that in international politics moral values should be decisive only in questions of last resort.[9] Similarly, former secretary of state Dean Acheson has suggested that "the vocabulary of morals and ethics is inadequate to discuss or test foreign policies of states." He argues that there are no moral standards of universal applicability that can be used by the diplomat. "What passes for ethical standards for governmental policies in foreign affairs," says Acheson, "is a collection of moralisms, maxims, and slogans, which neither

---

[9]Schlesinger, "Necessary Amorality," p. 72.

help nor guide, but only confuse, decision on such complicated matters. . . ."[10]

George Kennan, one of the most influential contemporary authors on foreign affairs, has expressed in several
writings[11] his skepticism about the contribution that moral
standards can make to foreign affairs. Fundamentally, Kennan argues that morality contributes little to foreign policy
because (1) there are no internationally accepted standards
of morality that can be used in promoting foreign policy
aims, and (2) the decisions of governments must be based
on principles other than personal morality. Kennan writes:

> Moral principles have their place in the heart of the
> individual and in the shaping of his own conduct,
> whether as a citizen or as a government official. . . . But
> when the individual's behavior passes through the ma-
> chinery of political organization and merges with that of
> millions of other individuals to find its expression in the
> actions of a government, then it undergoes a general
> transmutation, and the same moral concepts are no longer
> relevant to it. A government is an agent, not a principal;
> and no more than any other agent may it attempt to be the
> conscience of its principal. In particular, it may not subject
> itself to those supreme laws of renunciation and self-
> sacrifice that represent the culmination of individual
> moral growth.[12]

Like other realists, Kennan suggests that the only legitimate
basis of foreign policy is the national interest—which he
defines chiefly in terms of national security, the integrity of
political life, and the well-being of citizens. These interests,
he observes, have no moral quality but arise from the
decentralized character of international order.

The problem with Kennan's argument is that it is based
on an instrumental view of politics—a perspective that
assumes that the process of government is a "practical
exercise," not a moral one. The purpose of government,

[10]Dean Acheson, "Ethics in International Relations Today," *Vital Speeches of the Day*, Feb. 1, 1965, p. 227.

[11]The primary writings by George Kennan on ethics and foreign policy are: *American Diplomacy, 1900–1950* (New York: Mentor Books, 1963), pp. 82–89; *Realities of American Foreign Policy* (New York: Norton, 1966), pp. 47–50; and "Morality and Foreign Policy," *Foreign Affairs*, Winter 1985–86, pp. 205–18.

[12]Kennan, *Realities*, p. 48.

however, is not simply to limit conflict and restrain the selfishness of human beings; these are important government tasks, but not the only ones. The chief purpose of government is much nobler. Government, as a divinely ordained institution, is called to promote justice, peace, and human dignity. The responsibilities of the state are, therefore, both positive and negative, moral and instrumental.

A second limitation of Kennan's analysis is that it assumes that the only useful morality is one that is explicit, concrete, and specific—one that provides categorical imperatives for human decisions. But complex human endeavors, whether in business, law, or politics, cannot be based on simple moral choices. Morality consists not in fixed rules of right and wrong but in broad principles that guide and inform human choices. To be relevant, principles do not have to provide categorical directives. Their function in foreign affairs is not to provide simple ethical verdicts to the complex issues of trade, military defense, foreign aid, etc., but to mold and reform the general conception of the state's fundamental interests and to illuminate morally acceptable methods of promoting them. For example, the rudimentary principles of justice, freedom, order, human dignity, and political equality do not provide explicit guidance for people, but their embryonic character does not mean that they are not recognized and applied. There is ample evidence that government officials and students of foreign affairs are aware of their existence. Kenneth Thompson notes:

> States in formulating their foreign policies seek points of correspondence between what they do and the broader principle. In foreign policy the concept of elemental right and wrong is never fully realized, but it can be approximated. Even the fact that states possess an awareness of injustice indicates the possibility of justice in foreign affairs, for a sense of injustice presupposes categories of justice to which leaders have recourse.[13]

In short, moral principles provide general guidelines for human action. While the morality of international relations is more difficult to discern and apply than personal ethics, it is nonetheless authoritative and binding.

---

[13]Thompson, *Moral Issue*, p. 77.

THE AIMS OF MORALITY

If ethical standards are to be effectively applied to the making and implementation of a sound, coherent foreign policy, it is important to understand what moral norms can and cannot do. Moral norms make three important contributions to U.S. foreign policy.

Direction

First, ethical norms provide a focus and direction for the expression of the nation's major international goals. Statesmen generally define the fundamental foreign policy objectives of a nation as the national interest. The aim of ethical norms is not, however, to give specific guidance to a statesman on specific problems in foreign affairs, but rather to provide direction to the general character of foreign affairs. Arthur Schlesinger, Jr., has observed that the major purpose of morality is to "clarify and civilize conceptions of national interest."[14] Similarly, theologian John C. Bennett has written that Christian faith and ethics "offer ultimate perspectives, broad criteria, motives, inspirations, sensitivities, warnings, moral limits rather than directives for policies and decisions."[15]

Moral norms can also serve as a beacon, as a light guiding a ship through the stormy waters of world politics. If there is no vision, no reference point, diplomacy will lack consistency and continuity and will be hopelessly tossed to and fro by the conflicting interests in domestic and international politics. Henry Kissinger has written:

> It is not possible to conduct a foreign policy without a vision of the world that one wants to bring about, some definition of what one means by peace, and by justice and by order and by stability and by progress. If one does not have that vision, one runs the risk of a series of unrelated decisions.[16]

---

[14] Arthur Schlesinger, Jr., "National Interests and Moral Absolutes," in Ernest W. Lefever, ed., *Ethics and World Politics* (Baltimore: Johns Hopkins University Press, 1972), p. 35.

[15] John C. Bennett, *Foreign Policy in Christian Perspective* (New York: Scribner, 1966), p. 36.

[16] Henry Kissinger, "The Realities of Security," *AEI Foreign Policy and Defense Review*, vol. 3, no. 6 (1982), p. 11.

If a state is to pursue a moral foreign policy, it will need standards by which to assess its own debates and actions.

For the Christian the foundational norms of action are rooted in the Scriptures, but neither the Bible nor Christian ethics is sufficient to provide answers to such issues as trade policy, strategic arms limitation talks, South African apartheid, or illegal immigration. Indeed, the aim of moral norms is not to provide specific solutions, but to establish a direction and context that can result in moral action. Many years ago the famous eighteenth-century parliamentarian Edmund Burke, in comparing the role of the statesman and the moralist, observed that the statesman was not someone who disregarded ethics, but rather was a decision maker who applied ethics to specific problems. In Burke's words, he was a person who, "having a general view of society and the principles by which it is to be guided, would base his decision on the circumstances, yet never losing sight of the principles by which he is to be guided."[17] Christians concerned with foreign policy need to heed Burke's advice. They need to develop a firm grasp of fundamental biblical principles and then apply them with care and wisdom.

Judgment

Second, moral principles serve as a basis—a plumb line—for assessing foreign policy. Moral norms provide an independent, transcendent standard for judging human actions and choices. Without morality, foreign policy succumbs to the game of power politics, where the standard of right is defined by military might. Moral norms are thus important in providing a basis for judging the actions and policies of other states.

An even more significant contribution of morality is that it provides the basis for self-judgment. All human beings are proud and self-centered and use morality to justify their actions. Given the selfishness of persons and the egotism of nations, the most difficult moral challenge is to apply transcendent norms to proximate situations—circumstances in which we are directly involved. It is much easier to judge others than to judge ourselves. And this is partly why the balanced application of morality to foreign affairs is so difficult to achieve. The English historian Herbert Butterfield

---

[17] Quoted in Schlesinger, "Necessary Amorality," pp. 75–76.

has observed that the cause of morality is furthered insofar as self-judgment is applied to human choices.[18] Similarly, Reinhold Niebuhr has written that there can be no moral action without self-criticism, and no self-criticism without the capacity of self-transcendence.[19]

The requirement of self-criticism does not mean that we should disregard the evils of foreign governments and that we should take no account of the moral legitimacy of other regimes. The aim of morality is to provide a basis for evaluating our own behavior and that of others as well, but because of the selfish and sinful nature of people, a moral public policy must begin with self-judgment and, where appropriate, repentance, rather than with the assessment of others.

The unbalanced application of morality to U.S. foreign policy has historically contributed to either isolationism or imperialism. The first is the result of applying morality exclusively within national borders; the second is the consequence of applying moral norms solely to foreign countries. Both are manifestations of selfish behavior—the first for having an extreme pride in weakness and limited responsibility, the second for having an extreme pride in omnipotence and moral virtue. The challenge in applying transcendent norms is to avoid such extremes. Hans Morgenthau has written about the difficulty in finding the appropriate balance between such extremes:

> We have no choice between power and the common good. To act successfully, that is, according to the rules of the political art, is political wisdom. To know with despair that the political act is inevitably evil, and to act nevertheless, is moral courage. To choose among several expedient actions the least evil one is moral judgment. In the combination of political wisdom, moral courage, and moral judgment, man reconciles his political nature with moral destiny.[20]

---

[18] Herbert Butterfield, *International Conflict in the Twentieth Century* (New York: Harper and Brothers, 1960), pp. 23–25.

[19] Reinhold Niebuhr, *Moral Man and Immoral Society* (New York: Scribner, 1960), pp. 88–89.

[20] Hans J. Morgenthau, *Scientific Man Versus Power Politics* (Chicago: University of Chicago Press, 1965), p. 203.

Inspiration

Finally, moral norms are important because they inspire and mobilize action. Developing emotional appeal is especially important in democratic societies since the long-term effectiveness of any policy will be determined in large part by continuing public support. Leaders have the responsibility for initiating policy, but if its implementation is to be effective, it will have to capture the imagination of the public. One of the reasons why the memory of John F. Kennedy still lingers in the cities, towns, and villages of the Third World is that Kennedy's moral idealism—his articulation of America's vision of peace, justice, and human progress—captured the imagination and admiration of millions of citizens in the developing nations. The dynamic start of the Peace Corps in the early 1960s is but one evidence of the impact of Kennedy's idealistic vision on the collegiate youth of North America.

THE DANGERS OF MORALITY

One of the dangers in explicitly applying ethical norms to foreign policy is that it can lead to the misuse of moral norms. This danger, amply demonstrated in the annals of U.S. diplomacy, has been expressed by overzealous, self-righteous leaders whose moralistic policies have eventually discredited the values that were ostensibly being promoted. If Christians are to help develop a more moral U.S. foreign policy, they need to guard against some of the sins of their forefathers. The following four dangers in particular need to be avoided.

Moralism

The danger of moralism results from the application of simplistic moral stereotypes to complex foreign problems. Moralism results both from an oversimplification of problems and from a perversion of moral reasoning. The oversimplification of issues derives, in great measure, from the use of simplistic ideological perspectives that distort international realities. As Schlesinger has pointed out, ideology is the curse of public affairs "because it converts politics into a branch of theology and sacrifices human beings at the altar of

abstractions."[21] Some world conflicts can, of course, be
defined in simple terms, but most cannot. And the eagerness
of interest groups and political leaders to promote peace and
justice internationally places special burdens on those who
are responsible for developing morally prudent policies to
cope with the complex realities of world politics.

There can be no doubt, for example, that the movement
of international communism has played a vital role in the
evolution of Nicaragua since the Sandinistas came to power
in 1979. But it is equally clear that the problems of Central
America do not involve only East-West ideological issues, as
some have suggested, or only problems of economic injustice, as others have stated. Like all social reality, the conflicts
in Central America are complex, and it is unwise to apply
simple moral verdicts to such issues. In applying ethics in
foreign affairs it is wise, then, to recall H. L. Menchen's view
that "for every complex problem there is a simple solution—
and it is always wrong."

Moralism also results from the oversimplification of
ethics. The Bible provides numerous basic norms that can be
applied to the conduct of foreign relations. Some of these
will be explored in the following chapter. Interpreting
biblical revelation, however, is difficult, and there is no
consensus among Christian theologians and ethicists about
which principles constitute an appropriate framework for
public policy.

Since it is impossible to reduce Christian ethics or
traditional Western morality to a settled hierarchy of norms,
the explicit application of morality to foreign policy will
inevitably lead to an apparent conflict among ethical values.
The decision maker will then be forced to discriminate
among equally legitimate moral standards. The moralist
seeks to avoid such morally ambiguous situations by denying some legitimate norms and becoming exclusively at-
tached to one or two of them. The advocate of peace at any
price or the defender of free enterprise who refuses to
recognize the public responsibilities for the poor and the
aged exemplify such moralism. The application of simplistic
moral slogans is not only harmful, but discredits the
legitimate role that ethical norms and moral reasoning can

---

[21]Arthur Schlesinger, Jr., "The Two Faces of American Foreign Policy,"
Sunday Sun-Times [Chicago], Oct. 16, 1983, p. 6.

play in foreign affairs. The search for moral purity and simplicity in world affairs cannot be overcome by developing simplistic ideologies or denying moral choice. All domestic and foreign problems involve overlapping and even competing moral norms, and the problem faced by the statesman is how to develop a prudent policy based among various moral alternatives.

One of the most destructive effects of moralism in world politics is that it breeds intense conflicts among states. When statesmen cease to be diplomats and become crusaders for their nation's special interests, they increase the intensity of world conflicts and impede the quest for international peace. Hans Morgenthau has observed in his classic text, *Politics Among Nations*, that

> the morality of the particular group, far from limiting the struggle for power on the international scene, gives the struggle a ferocity and intensity not known to other ages. For the claim to universality which inspires the moral code of one particular group is incompatible with the identical claim of another group; the world has room for only one, and the other must yield or be destroyed.[22]

The truth of Morgenthau's assessment is borne out by the current religious war between Iran and Iraq—a war which in five years has claimed nearly a million lives.

Self-Righteousness

The second major danger arises from over-confidence in one's own moral rectitude. To a large degree, self-righteousness arises from the failure to apply authentic morality to our own and our nation's life. States, of course, seek to clothe their interests and actions in universalistic moral language. They do so in order to legitimize interests by gaining public approval, not to bring moral judgment to bear on the interests and actions.

Self-righteousness also results from the simplistic application of morality to complex issues. But moral purity is impossible in foreign affairs; there is no perfect method of reconciling the claims of justice with the necessities of power in the world. Foreign policy is, and must be, morally ambiguous—both because we cannot fully know the mind of

---

[22]Morgenthau, *Man Versus Politics*, p. 263.

the Creator and also because we do not live in accord with the Creator's mandates. As Christians, we do affirm the existence of absolute norms, but it is one thing to affirm their existence and quite another to give concrete expression to them. "What is desperately needed," says Paul Henry, "is the moral humility to accept the fact that while God's standards are absolute and unchanging, we as individuals are never able to know or apply them with perfection."[23]

One of the unfortunate results of self-righteousness is hypocrisy, the pretentious use of moral slogans for national gain. This problem arises from the confusion between principles, which may be just and correct, and behavior, which often is not. Since all political activity is partly an exercise in self-interest, there can be no wholly just or moral nation or perfect foreign policy. All political endeavors, no matter how inspired they are by transcendent norms, are unable to overcome human finiteness. This is especially true for states, which are notorious instruments of national selfishness.

Reinhold Niebuhr has suggested that, because egotism is especially pronounced in nations, one of the dominant moral features of states is their hypocrisy. The reason for this, according to Niebuhr, is that nations are less able than individuals to "behold the beam that is in their own eye while they observe the mote that is in their brother's eye; and individuals find it difficult enough."[24] But nations are not self-righteous simply because they fail to be self-critical. They are self-righteous because they seek to clothe their interests in moral language and thereby gain universal public approval. British writers during the late nineteenth century, for example, argued that free trade was conducive to economic growth and to peace, but their justification of such beliefs was not unrelated to the fact that Britain, a dominant imperial power at that time, was the chief beneficiary of such policies.[25] Similarly, U.S. interventions in Central America, while generally justified in terms of the economic and political welfare of indigenous peoples, were also carried out for geopolitical purposes. Morality was not the sole or even primary motivation of Washington decision makers.

---

[23] Paul Henry, *Politics for Evangelicals* (Valley Forge: Judson, 1974), p. 74.
[24] Niebuhr, *Moral Man*, p. 107.
[25] Carr, *Twenty Years' Crisis*, pp. 54–60.

It is important to distinguish here between the absolutist, relativist, and the principled pragmatist. The absolutist assumes that he or she can know and apply God's ethics; the relativist denies the existence of the Creator and of his moral laws, believing that truth is flexible and relative to time and place. The principled pragmatist affirms the existence of absolute, unchanging moral norms but believes that, because of human finiteness, people must apply them with humility and tentativeness.

Since foreign policy is complex, thoughtful Christians will disagree on the nature of both problems and their solutions. For example, some Christians have been of the opinion that a major cause of the arms race is the continued application of technology to nuclear deterrence. For such people, the strategic defense initiative (S.D.I.) is a wrong, evil policy. By contrast, other Christians believe that the condition of mutual assured destruction (M.A.D.), which has governed U.S.–U.S.S.R. strategic nuclear relations during the past two decades, is immoral. For such persons, S.D.I. provides a means out of the allegedly immoral policy of M.A.D. Who is right? Is continuation of reliance on strategic offense without defense better that moving toward a primarily defensive nuclear strategy? How are we to know the mind of God on issues such as these?

There are limits to moral knowledge, and Christians especially need to ponder the wisdom offered by Abraham Lincoln during the Civil War when he was confronted by a group of Presbyterian ministers seeking to give him advice. In reply to the ministers' petition to emancipate all slaves immediately, Lincoln wrote:

> In the great contests each party claims to act in accordance with the will of God. Both may be and one must be wrong. God cannot be for and against the same thing at the same time. . . . I'm approached with the most opposite opinions and advice and that by religious men who are equally certain that they represent the divine will. I'm sure that either the one or the other class is mistaken in that belief and perhaps in some respects both. I hope it will not be irreverent for me to say that if it is probable that God would reveal his will to others on a point so connected with my duty it might be supposed he would reveal it directly to me. For unless I am more deceived in myself than I often am it is my earnest desire to know the

will of Providence in this matter and if I can learn what it will be I will do it. These are not, however, the days of miracles and I suppose it will be granted that I am not to expect a direct revelation. I must study the plain physical facts of the case, ascertain what is possible and learn what appears to be wise and right.[26]

Since the world is an environment with nations espousing profoundly different values, the development and implementation of U.S. foreign policy needs to be undertaken in the light of the multiplicity of ideologies and moral codes. The United States should guard against the sin of moral imperialism. Father Hesburgh of Notre Dame has written that, "despite all America's flaws . . . the simple fact is that America and its aspirations are still the best expression of what I would call mankind's universal hope."[27] I believe that Father Hesburgh is right, but in the light of twentieth-century international relations, such a conviction is exceedingly dangerous, for Americans may begin to assume moral superiority. Indeed, to the extent that they develop a conviction about their unique role in world affairs, they weaken the qualities that have made the American democratic experiment an inspiration. Moreover, few states are eager to have their national identity molded by another state. The bedrock of international community is the sovereignty of states. This is why Stanley Hoffmann, in *Duties Beyond Borders*, says that an essential norm of the international community of states is moderation, or what he terms "the morality of self-restraint."[28]

Cynicism

One of the dangers of national hypocrisy is that it can lead to cynicism—that is, the denial of transcendent standards. When moral norms are used pretentiously and self-righteously, the results can be catastrophic. Not only is public policy jeopardized, but the very existence of God's transcendent reality will be questioned and denied. Christians, therefore, need to be especially careful in justifying political preferences based on biblical and moral truths.

---

[26]Quoted in Morgenthau, *Man Versus Politics*, p. 263.

[27]Theodore M. Hesburgh and Louis Halle, *Foreign Policy & Morality* (New York: Council on Religion and International Affairs, 1979), p. 19.

[28]Stanley Hoffmann, *Duties Beyond Borders* (Syracuse: Syracuse University Press, 1981), p. 33.

Conflict among different ethical perspectives or moral values need not result in cynicism. Moral judgment is possible. During the Second World War, Archbishop William Temple observed that one major difference between the British and the Nazis was that the former did not practice what they preached, while the latter did.[29] Nor should conflict among competing moralities deny the existence of transcendent norms. Historian E. H. Carr says that the major contribution of political realists to the analysis of international relations is that they expose the weaknesses of idealists who profess to have identified universal moral norms. He writes:

> The exposure of the real basis of the professedly abstract principles commonly invoked in international politics is the most damning and most convincing part of the realist indictment of utopianism. . . . The charge is not that human beings fail to live up to their principles. . . . What matters is that these supposedly absolute and universal principles were not principles at all, but the unconscious reflections of national policy based on a particular interpretation of national interest at a particular time.[30]

While Carr correctly questions the moral legitimacy of utopian doctrines popular in nineteenth-century Europe, his fundamental critique is not a denial of transcendence but of the misuse of morality. The tragedy is not that principles cannot and should not be applied, but rather that selfishness can be easily clothed in morality. The professed principles articulated by British elites were not moral principles at all.

This study is based on the conviction that ethical norms in general and Christian values in particular can be applied, if imperfectly, to the conduct of foreign affairs. Indeed, Christians have a special responsibility to affirm, in the midst of the cynicism and moral confusion of the world, biblical truths and norms by which the world can be made more peaceful and just. But if the affirmation and application of ethics to diplomacy is to contribute to the building of a better world, Christians will have to carry out their task with sensitivity and tentativeness, lest their moral zeal lead them to self-righteous moralism.

---

[29] Quoted in Bennett, *Foreign Policy*, p. 13.
[30] Carr, *Twenty Years' Crisis*, p. 87.

Neglecting Consequences

A final danger in the explicit application of morality is the exclusive focus on intentions and the neglect of consequences. As noted earlier, political idealism emphasizes intentions, while political realism emphasizes the consequences of actions. The problem with applying moral norms to foreign policy is that it can lead to an overconcern with motives, intentions, and goals. Since moral purity is far easier to achieve in thought than in deed, there is a natural tendency to be philosophical and theoretical in dealing with morality. But while the purity of motives is important in religion, it is not the deciding factor in politics. The aim of morality is not to purify goals, but to uplift the quality of life—to bring peace and justice to this world. A morality that provides direction and vision is important, but vision alone is not enough. Morality should address the institutional structures that promote justice. It should examine the political and economic institutions of nations and of international organizations and assess the consequences of the various institutions.

One clue as to how Christians can avoid the confusion over political intentions and consequences is found in the political history of the United States. The founding of the American republic illustrates the role of ethics in providing both vision and structure, goals and institutions. The ideals and noble aspirations that inspired the founding of the United States are expressed in the Declaration of Independence. This brief idealistic statement articulates the purposes, goals, and ideals that are to serve as the ultimate source of national purpose. Had the founding of the republic relied solely on the inspiration of this document, however, the American democratic experiment would have failed long ago.

The second indispensable element of the American political system is the U.S. Constitution. If the Declaration was inspired by an optimistic vision of humankind, the U.S. Constitution was the work of realists like James Madison and Alexander Hamilton, who believed that a limited government could only be maintained by the creation of institutional arrangements. The great genius of the American founding fathers is not that they had more noble dreams than their predecessors, but rather that they had the wisdom to apply principles of checks and balances and separation of powers to the creation of institutions designed to serve moral ends. The genius was in applying morality to institutions. The moral aspirations articulated in 1776 are of course important in that they provide inspiration and direction for the nation. Yet the wisdom inherent in the Constitution has, as the late Martin Diamond observed, "been the necessary forming, constraining and sustaining system of government which has made our revolution a blessing to mankind and not a curse."[31]

The danger in explicitly applying moral norms to the conduct of diplomacy is that it can easily result in an idealistic program of world peace and justice. Many writers, both secular and Christian, have recommended a new world system, with drastically reformed institutions. It is easy to contemplate a better world order. But Christians must do more than dream; we must work to make the world system we live in more just and humane. We must build and maintain institutions that promote and sustain human dignity.

[31] Martin Diamond, "The Revolution of Sober Expectations" in *The American Revolution: Three Views* (New York: American Brands, 1975), p. 84.

2

CHRISTIANITY AND FOREIGN POLICY

"When the political and social ideas used by Christians today are identified and analyzed, it becomes clear that they are derived from secular values of the time."

Edward Norman[1]

"When the sacred tenets of faith and the highest moral values cherished by Christian believers are involved in a public issue, the subject deserves to be treated not in a vain catchphrase political polemicism but with balanced integrity of thought and respect bordering on reverence for others as well as for the truth which one hopes to clarify by posing hard questions."

James Dougherty[2]

During the past three decades Christians throughout the world have become more involved in domestic and international affairs. The increasing political activity of churches has been especially felt in the United States, where religious elites of mainline Protestant and Catholic churches have been deeply involved in the major public political debates of the nation. Beginning with the Vietnam War in the late

---

[1] Edward Norman, *Christianity and the World Order* (Oxford: Oxford University Press, 1979), p. 72.

[2] James Dougherty, *The Bishops and Nuclear Weapons* (Hamden, Conn.: Archon Books, 1984), p. 17.

1960s, church groups have lobbied for a variety of international causes, including arms control; Third World development; human rights in authoritarian countries, especially in South Africa; nuclear strategy; and most recently, aid to Central America.

In the late 1970s a major development occurred in the evolution of American religious politics: the Fundamentalists and Evangelicals awakened to their domestic and international political responsibilities and became deeply involved in the 1980 presidential campaign and significant public policy issues. The rise of evangelical politics is important because it has challenged many of the political views articulated by the mainline Protestant and Catholic churches. In recent years the political agenda of mainline Protestant churches has associated prophetic politics with a liberal political agenda and has, among other things, identified God's justice with a decline in U.S. military and political power in the world, supported the influence and expansion of international governmental institutions, defended revolutionary causes in developing nations, and promoted socialism as an appropriate vehicle for economic development. By contrast, the politically active Fundamentalists and conservative Evangelicals, known as the Religious Right, have tended to identify the Christian faith with a strong defense policy, a vigorous support of democracy, opposition to communism, and support of regimes friendly to the United States, even when the government is controlled by the military. For example, while many mainline Protestant churches have been openly critical of regimes in Chile, South Africa, and South Korea, they have been relatively quiet about abuses in Cuba, Nicaragua, and the Soviet Union. The more conservative Christians, by contrast, have supported authoritarian regimes[3] but have been deeply critical of radical revolutionary regimes, such as in Nicaragua.

The increase in political activity among Christians, whether of liberal or conservative ideological inclinations,

---

[3] For example, Jerry Falwell, leader of the Moral Majority, after visiting South Africa and the Philippines in the fall of 1985, expressed support for regimes. He indicated that, while he opposed apartheid, he believed Prime Minister Botha's government to be making significant reforms. According to media reports, Falwell referred to the Philippines as "a paradise" and "one of the best friends the U.S. has in the world" (*New York Times*, Nov. 13, 1985).

has been a beneficial development. The Christian faith has implications not only for individuals, but also for community life at the national and international levels. The increased participation is significant because it provides a means by which Christians can carry the leaven of the kingdom of heaven into all areas of life, including the social, political, and economic structures of the world.

Along with the increasing involvement of Christians in international affairs has come a deeply disturbing development—namely, the politicization of faith. By politicization of faith I do not mean an expansion of religious political activity, but rather the transformation of faith itself into a more political and social gospel. Edward Norman, in his 1978 Reith Lectures, has defined this new faith as "a scheme of social and political action, dependent . . . upon supernatural authority for its ultimate claims to attention, but rendered in categories that are derived from the political theories and practices of contemporary society."[4] Norman goes on to observe that while there are a variety of different expressions of this new politicized religion, they all start from "a rejection of preceding Christian attitudes, from a belief that Christians have in the past been too concerned with spirituality."[5]

We can agree with Norman that the increased effort to identify the gospel with a particular political agenda has been detrimental to religion. It has weakened the moorings of authentic faith and has left the church to be tossed around in the turbulent seas of contemporary world politics. We can also agree that the identification of religious politics with a liberal and revolutionary political ideology has been especially detrimental to the church because it has distorted priorities and has identified transcendent norms with a limited and inadequate set of political and economic ideals and institutions. Because of their affinities with particular institutions and regimes, the churches have lost their prophetic power to pass judgment on all norms and institutions in society and in the world. According to Norman, "the Christian religion has lost the power, and also the

---

[4]Norman, *Christianity and World Order*, p. 2.
[5]Ibid.

confidence, to define the areas of public debate, even in moral questions."[6]

While Norman correctly assesses the nature and character of the increasingly politicized faith of the church, his remedy of encouraging the "privitization" of faith[7] is not only inadequate, but unbiblical. The Christian religion is, of course, fundamentally about the relationship of God to people, but authentic faith is expressed not only by individuals through worship and faithfulness to God's laws, but also through the communal witness of the church. Christian witness is individual and collective. Richard Mouw has correctly observed that redemption is partly political, requiring the transformation and reform of the social and political institutions of society.[8] To be sure, the task of political evangelism—that is, the infiltration of the temporal political and economic order with the love of God—must be undertaken with the greatest care and humility, lest such efforts distort true faith. The complexity and difficulty of this mission does not, however, absolve Christians from the responsibility of fulfilling the redemption mandate.

The major problem of a politicized faith, then, is not that Christians are applying faith to public policies, but rather that they are doing so in a careless and irresponsible fashion. The increasing involvement of Christians in foreign policy debates is not wrong, but the uncritical integration of faith with secular political ideology is. This study assumes that the problems of politicized religion are not a consequence of Christian political involvement per se, but the result of a careless and uncritical integration of religion and politics. What is needed, in short, is not less political activity among Christians, but a more responsible and faithful witness.

If Christians are to contribute to the making and implementation of a moral and humane U.S. foreign policy on the basis of their faith, they will have to develop a sound social ethic based on the Scriptures and a strategy by which biblical principles can be applied to the concrete problems of world affairs.

There are three specific obstacles that must be overcome in developing and implementing a Christian approach to

---

[6] Ibid., p. 4.
[7] Ibid., p. 80.
[8] Richard J. Mouw, *Political Evangelism* (Grand Rapids: Eerdmans, 1973), ch. 1.

foreign policy. First, fundamental moral problems of world politics and U.S. diplomacy must be identified and defined. There can be no responsible Christian influence in foreign affairs if the participants in the public debate are uninformed about issues or unaware of alternative policy proposals. Second, Christians must identify and define key scriptural principles relating to public affairs. The challenge here is both substantive and hermeneutical, for the development of such principles requires a thorough knowledge of the Bible and the identification of an appropriate approach to its interpretation and application. Finally, an effective Christian political witness will require an appropriate strategy, especially as it relates to the conduct of world affairs.

In this chapter I shall deal with the last two obstacles. First, I shall identify and explain a number of key biblical norms that should inform and direct any individual or collective political efforts of Christians. Second, I shall describe some essential features of a faithful and responsible strategy of political evangelism. In subsequent chapters I shall describe and analyze a number of key problems in world politics, providing some suggestions for the promotion of public justice.

BIBLICAL FRAMEWORK

Is there a biblical perspective on world politics? Are there biblical principles that can guide the development and implementation of a just and moral U.S. foreign policy? The Bible is not a manual for public policy. It does not provide specific guidance for developing an alternative world system or for solving the problems of U.S. foreign policy. The Bible does provide, however, general principles that can and should guide the efforts of Christians seeking to influence world affairs in general and U.S. foreign policy in particular. These principles will not provide solutions for complex foreign policy problems, such as deterrence, apartheid, world poverty, and international peacekeeping; but they will offer a framework by which foreign policy issues can be assessed. While the scope of this study does not allow a full elaboration of biblical norms, I want to examine briefly three principles that must be applied in any moral assessment of foreign policy. These three foundational principles are God's sovereignty and love, the universality and totality of sin, and the call to biblical justice.

God's Sovereignty and Love

The first major principle is this: God is a sovereign, omnipotent, and omniscient ruler whose power extends to all peoples and all nations throughout time. All creation lives under the providence and judgment of God. The prophet Isaiah captures the greatness of God in the midst of world affairs in the following words:

> Surely the nations are like a drop in a bucket;
>   they are regarded as dust on the scales;
>   he weighs the islands as though they were fine
>   dust. . . .
> He sits enthroned above the circle of the earth,
>   and its people are like grasshoppers.
> He stretches out the heavens like a canopy,
>   and spreads them out like a tent to live in.
> He brings princes to naught
>   and reduces the rulers of this world to nothing.
>   (Isa. 40:15, 22–23)

God is the Creator and Sustainer of life, the Lord of history, and the Redeemer of humankind. Although God is sovereign over all peoples and states, he uses human beings to accomplish his purposes in the world. This is why Christians, as God's children, must be obedient in promoting his righteousness and justice within the world community. Finally, nations live under the judgment of God. God's standards for individuals and nations are his justice and righteousness. While God's love is total and universal, the Scriptures teach that God holds individuals and nations accountable for their behavior. Because human beings do not and cannot live in perfect harmony with the Creator, they fall short of fulfilling the divine mandate. In the words of the apostle Paul, they "fall short of the glory of God" (Rom. 3:23). The only healing that can come to people is through the recognition and admission of their sin and through repentance. The Scriptures remind us of the importance of collective repentance: "If my people, who are called by my name, will humble themselves and pray and seek my face and turn from their wicked ways, then will I hear from heaven and will forgive their sin and will heal their land" (2 Chron. 7:14).

Another important implication of God's sovereignty is that he loves all peoples and all nations. Because of the universality and totality of his love, he has no favorites. Since all nations are under his control and judgment, some Christians have interpreted the universality of God's love and sovereignty to mean that the ideal form of world organization is a world federal state. While a central government would have a distinct advantage over the existing decentralized political order in the resolution of interstate disputes, the concentration of political power in one world government would pose an enormous threat to the political freedom and dignity of people worldwide. Since one of the major impediments to human dignity throughout history has been the tyranny of governments, the centralization of political power in one world regime would pose the most dangerous threat to human history in the annals of civilization. Thus the dilemma of world order (explored in chapter 3) is how to promote it while also maintaining pluralism and a decentralized political system. As I shall argue later on, the existing world order is imperfect in that it provides no effective mechanism for resolving disputes among states. At the same time, the dispersion of political power among two superpowers and some 160 other states provides an environment that inhibits the centralization of political power.

The Reality of Sin

A second major biblical principle concerns the view of human nature. The Bible teaches that the cause of injustice, conflict, and unrighteousness is rooted not in social and political structures, but in the nature of people themselves. It is a mistake, however, to view human nature as totally evil and depraved. If people were totally evil, there would be no possibility of community or even of a modicum of justice and peace. More importantly, such a view does not accord with biblical teaching. The Bible teaches that man was created in the image of God, an image which is present in all persons and which is the source of good. But the Scriptures also teach that people are alienated from God by virtue of human sin and rebellion against him. Human rebellion, made possible by the freedom to choose, is manifested by self-love and pride that lead people into open hostility with God and to enthrone another god—self. Human rebellion, however, does not involve a total corruption of human essence, but only estrangement and alienation from God. Estrangement does not mean that people have lost all of God's image, but rather that their original nature has become perverted.[9]

According to the Bible, the corruption of human nature is universal and total. It is universal in that it affects all people regardless of nationality, race, or social class (Rom. 3:23); and it is total in that it affects all of a person's being— his mind, body, and soul. Because of the pervasiveness and universality of sin, human beings can never act wholly justly and righteously, even when they do so in the name of God. All people bear the fruit of sin and human corruption. Even the most noble, lofty, and idealistic expressions of justice cannot escape the shortcomings of human finiteness.

President Reagan, in addressing the National Association of Evangelicals' annual convention in 1983, provided a good summary of the problem of sin in world affairs. He observed: "There is sin and evil in the world. And we are enjoined by scripture and the Lord Jesus to oppose it with all our might. Our nation, too, has a legacy of evil with which it must deal."[10]

Justice

The third biblical principle is this: God's standard for judging political communities is justice. One of the important lessons of the Old Testament is that God chose a political community—the nation of Israel—to bring about his will. The Israelites, of course, were not always obedient to God, and the prophets' task was to warn them about the coming judgment on their unfaithfulness and injustice.

Defining biblical justice is not easy. To begin with, identifying and defining transcendent norms applicable to imperfect and transitory temporal political rules and institutions is a most difficult task. The problem is that any temporal efforts to relate transcendent norms to temporal definitions will be woefully inadequate. Moreover, since the

---

[9]For a thorough exploration of this point, see Reinhold Niebuhr's *The Nature and Destiny of Man*, vol. 1 (New York: Scribner, 1964), especially ch. 10.

[10]Office of Media Relations and Planning, *Remarks of the President to the 41st Annual Convention of the National Association of Evangelicals*, March 8, 1983, p. 6.

Scriptures do not present a clear, comprehensive definition of justice, theologians are not agreed as to exactly what constitutes the biblical teaching about justice. The Old Testament provides a well-developed conception of justice based on law. The New Testament, by contrast, says little about justice and instead focuses primarily on the love of God as expressed in the redemptive work of Christ. If we are to develop a biblical conception of justice, it must be based on the entire biblical revelation, and this means that the teachings of the Old and New Testament must be integrated.

The Old Testament notion of justice is best defined by *shalom*—the vision of a just peace articulated in the poetic and prophetic books. As Nicholas Wolterstorff has noted, *shalom* "is a human being dwelling at peace in all his or her relationships: with God, with self, with fellows, with nature."[11] King David described it as follows:

> Love and faithfulness meet together;
> righteousness and peace kiss each other.
>
> (Ps. 85:10)

The prophet Isaiah describes the *shalom* ideal as:

> ". . . to loose the chains of injustice
> and untie the cords of the yoke,
> to set the oppressed free
> and break every yoke[.]
> . . . to share your food with the hungry
> and to provide the poor wanderer with shelter—
> when you see the naked, to clothe him,
> and not to turn away from your own flesh and
> blood[.]"
>
> (58:6–7)

Fundamentally, the Old Testament teaching assumes that the only lasting foundation for peace is through reconciliation to God. Peace with God makes possible just and peaceful relationships within the family, neighborhood, state, and the world itself.

The New Testament focus on love is directly related to a vision of authentic justice. Love, of course, is not justice. Love involves unqualified giving, while justice involves calculation, measurement, and judgment. Emil Brunner once

---

[11]Nicholas Wolterstorff, *Until Justice and Peace Embrace* (Grand Rapids: Eerdmans, 1983), p. 70.

observed that love is always just but that justice is not necessarily love.[12] Love, in other words, is much broader, more encompassing than justice. As the dominant message of the New Testament, the commands to love God and our neighbor provide the basis for a just and peaceful political order. But political communities cannot operate solely in terms of the ethic of love, for the wants of people are unlimited and the resources are scarce. The problem of all political communities is how to allocate scarce resources fairly, and the standard of love is inadequate for carrying out this task.

A biblical conception of justice needs to be based on both the Old Testament vision of *shalom* and the New Testament teachings concerning God's love. The Old Testament vision of justice is important because it provides a transcendent standard by which the affairs of people can be judged. Brunner has noted that nothing can be measured with an elastic yardstick. "It is true," he writes, "that all social systems which we human beings create are only relatively just. But even such a relatively just system is only possible if we are guided by an idea of absolute justice, if we align what we build by the plummet of divine justice."[13] The vision of *shalom* is therefore essential to a Christian view of justice, for it provides the norm by which public institutions and policies are to be judged. There can be no injustice apart from a transcendent, divine morality.

The problem, of course, is that human beings are unable through their own initiatives to live according to the law. It is here where the love of God, through the redemptive work of Christ, provides a way of partially overcoming human sinfulness and finiteness and participating in the building of a more perfect and just world system. God's grace thus enables people to reach beyond the limited capabilities imposed by legalistic standards of justice. Rightly understood, the love of God provides the only foundation on which authentic justice can be built. Justice is not love, as we observed above, but it is the means by which it is implemented in the affairs of domestic and world politics. Indeed, justice is the vehicle by which love is expressed in the

---

[12] Emil Brunner, *Justice and the Social Order* (New York: Harper and Brothers, 1945), p. 261.
[13] Ibid., p. 9.

political process. In the words of Brunner, "justice is nothing but the form of love which has currency in the world of institutions."[14]

It is important to recognize that human conceptions of *shalom* will always be relative to time and place and contingent on particular circumstances.[15] But human finiteness need not paralyze Christian political action. Rather, by recognizing that all human efforts fall short of justice and perfection, Christians can articulate with humility and tentativeness a vision of *shalom*—a vision that can inspire and direct human efforts toward a more just and humane world system. Human efforts will be tainted with sin, but God's love and grace can enable human beings to partially overcome their moral limitations.

BIBLICAL APPLICATIONS

Implications of God's Sovereignty and Love

God's universal love means that a biblical foreign policy needs to take into account the interests of all peoples and all nations. One of the major obstacles to world harmony is excessive nationalism—the exaltation and idolatry of the nation. Americans have a moral responsibility to their own people, but the promotion of their own national interest should not be undertaken in disregard for or at the expense of the interests of other peoples. This does not mean that patriotism—the preference accorded to members of one's own community over those from distant communities—is morally wrong. Patriotism can be a salutary practice when it strengthens solidarity among people. But when patriotism becomes the highest good, then it becomes a hindrance to justice. North American Christians have a responsibility to support their nation and its government, but they also have a responsibility to peoples of other lands. Nationalism and patriotism should therefore not separate them from peoples living in distant lands.

Defining the boundaries of legitimate nationalism is not easy. It is especially difficult since Christians bear a triple allegiance—to the church (the body of Christ), the nation, and the world community. While the allegiance to God is

---

[14] Ibid., p. 261.
[15] Niebuhr, *Nature and Destiny of Man*, vol. 2, ch. 9.

absolute, it is not always clear how to appropriate the claims of each temporal community. The command of Jesus to give to Caesar the things that are Caesar's and to God the things that are God's is normative, but does not solve the problem of appropriating correctly our affinities in the myriad of conflicting situations that human beings confront on an ongoing basis. This is especially the case in defining legitimate allegiances to the nation and the world community.

It is always easy to critique nationalism and to affirm that patriotism has been a source of injustice. But what should be the moral claims of nations versus the international system? Should the United States, for example, be more concerned with its own national poverty or with the poverty in the Third World? How much food and economic aid should the American government give countries suffering from absolute hunger? Should the food and assistance be given to people or to governments? Does it matter? Should Christians advocate strong private and public transnational organizations and seek to transform the existing world order into a more harmonious world order? Or should they defend the existing world order and the high level of military expenditures that goes with it? Should the church support free trade even if it would result in unemployment in its own churches and parishes? Questions such as these are significant because they call attention to the moral ambiguity in defining the legitimate claims of nations and the world community. John C. Bennett and Harvey Seifert have written that "patriotism is a great good if it remains subordinate to goods that are higher and wider."[16] What makes the development of a moral foreign policy so challenging is that there are no clear definitions as to what are "higher" and "wider" goods.

The principle of God's love and sovereignty thus serves as a reminder of the universal context in which justice is to be undertaken. Because God loves the world, he has no favorites. And because his love and judgment are universal, an unlimited nationalism is morally unacceptable and contrary to biblical teaching. At the same time, an acceptable world order must protect the legitimate interests of all peoples and all nations.

[16]John C. Bennett and Harvey Seifert, *U.S. Foreign Policy and Christian Ethics* (Philadelphia: Westminster, 1977), p. 32.

Implications of Sin

There are three important implications of the biblical teaching about human nature to the affairs of international politics. First, because the centralization of power can lead to political tyranny, it is important to promote a pluralistic society and an institutional system inhibiting a monopoly of power. Domestically, pluralism and limited government can best be maintained through an institutional arrangement regime based on such principles as separation of powers, checks and balances, and periodic, competitive elections. Internationally, tyranny can best be prevented through a decentralized system of multiple centers of powers.

A major limitation of the existing world order is that states seek political security by relying on their own resources, especially military power. As a result, the international system feeds the disease of militarism. The effects of this disease are felt domestically in the exorbitant levels of military spending. Moreover, excessive reliance on military power for the protection of national sovereignty has resulted in politically powerful armed forces which periodically have been tempted to usurp civilian power and to establish their own rulers in power. This has been especially the case in Latin America and Africa. Internationally, excessive militarism has led to an arms race which in 1985 alone was estimated to cost all nations nearly $940 billion.[17]

Second, all proposals for making the world a more peaceful and just community must be based on a realistic assessment of human nature. Such an assessment must come to grips with the intensity and intractability of the world's political problems due to the totality and universality of sin. Church policy statements about issues such as war, famine, apartheid, and nuclear deterrence have often failed to address the underlying human conditions that are the root source of international conflicts and injustices. Kenneth Kantzer, for example, correctly questions the theological completeness of the Catholic bishops' pastoral letters on peace and the U.S. economy. Kantzer asks, "But whatever happened to sin?" He then observes that the U.S. Catholic bishops have forgotten to consider in their analyses the

---

[17] U.S. Arms Control and Disarmament Agency, *World Military Expenditures and Arms Transfers, 1985* (Washington, D.C.: ACDA Publication 123), p. 7.

impact of the doctrine of original sin in assessing and prescribing policies for the problems of war and poverty.[18]

A realistic approach to public policy must also come to grips with the limitations of any proposals and initiatives to promote justice. This admonition is especially appropriate for religious groups that attempt to clothe their recommendations in spiritual and moral language. The identification of faith with particular foreign policies can result in self-righteousness and moralism and fail to recognize human limitations as impediments to the discerning of God's will. Historically, religious groups, more than others, have been especially vulnerable to the illusion that reason, education, and morality can solve the world's political problems. But ideals and moral suasion are not sufficient. Indeed, their very presence can result in unrealistic and confused political thought.

Third, because all nations and all government policies are partly evil, foreign affairs need to be conducted with a high degree of "realism"—that is, an awareness of the fallen and imperfect nature of all actions, even those which are undertaken with the most noble of aspirations. It is important to recall that Jesus was most critical not of the publicans and sinners, but of the self-righteous leaders (the Pharisees) who prided themselves on their ability to teach and keep the law. Authentic faith does not derive from our inherent goodness, but from God's divine resources available through Jesus Christ. Self-judgment and repentance are the preconditions of moral behavior.

The Christian teachings about sin and confession can contribute to foreign policy by inhibiting moralism and self-righteousness. One of the ironies of international politics is that justice becomes most possible when individuals and nations recognize their inherent selfishness and propensity for self-righteousness. Herbert Butterfield has written eloquently of the dangers of self-righteousness in diplomacy:

> It is a paradox that the highest and most spiritual view of life which is available to man—and the one which carried human beings to the most elevated and rarefied realms of experience—is one which starts with the assertion of universal human sinfulness. The very ladder which has

---

[18]Kenneth S. Kantzer, "Pastoral Letters and the Realities of Life," *Christianity Today*, March 1, 1985, p. 13.

carried men to those exalted spheres and regions of light has an end which rests in the mundane realm on the primary recognition of this fact. The finest examples of human sainthood and the finest blossomings of human personality seem to emerge out of an initial abasement of the human being before this very truth. They seem indeed to be inseparable from a continuous confession of sin, and the very power which works with such efficacy in holy people is the knowledge of the forgiveness of sins.[19]

If public policy is to be undertaken in the name of the Lord, it will need to be based on a healthy dose of skepticism and tentativeness. Some of the greatest evils in world politics have been committed by people who have sought to act in the name of the Lord but have failed to take into consideration their own finiteness and sinfulness. Robert Goldwin observes that some of the most despicable tyrannies are borne of lofty ideals that become corrupted and twisted by political leaders; and that the greatest political achievement, a government of sustained, ordered liberty, is the result of humble aspirations. Because good government is born of a realistic human assessment, Goldwin believes that the promotion and protection of human dignity is best achieved by recognizing the "lowly" origin of political liberty and human rights.[20]

The biblical view of human nature provides both hope and caution to world affairs. Hope for a more just, humane world is possible precisely because God's image is implanted in people and can be further renewed in his likeness through the redemptive work of Christ. But because of sin, world affairs will always be imperiled by greed, exploitation, and war. Christians involved directly or indirectly in the making of U.S. foreign policy need to avoid the extremes of fatalism and sentimentalism, pessimism and romanticism. Paraphrasing Reinhold Niebuhr, we can affirm that man's capacity for justice makes world peace and harmony possible, but man's capacity for injustice makes prudent foreign policy necessary.

[19] Herbert Butterfield, *Christianity, Diplomacy and War* (New York: Abingdon-Cokesbury, 1953), p. 42.
[20] Robert Goldwin, "Human Rights and American Foreign Policy, Part IV—Arguments and Afterwards," *The Center Magazine*, July–Aug. 1984, p. 62.

Implications of Justice

One of the most intractable problems in applying the Bible to world affairs is to define and apply justice. What types of foreign policies, for example, can most effectively promote *shalom*? What institutions can promote international justice? What should be the United States' international priorities?

If Christians are to assess world affairs in terms of God's justice, they will need to have a clear operational conception of what justice is. The conception of biblical justice outlined earlier, based on the integration of the Old Testament vision of *shalom* with the New Testament command of love, provides an ideal standard, not an operational code, of the kingdom of God. It provides an orientation and direction for political action, not a gauge for judging international laws, international agreements, and transnational institutions. Moreover, even if the Scriptures did affirm an operational code of international justice, the application of such a code would present insuperable problems. It is one thing for God to define justice through his Word; it is quite another thing for finite human beings to apply such moral norms to concrete public political situations.

The inability to develop an operational definition of justice has led many thinkers to define justice instrumentally rather than substantively—that is, in terms of its means rather than of its goals or purposes. Paul Henry, an evangelical politician and scholar, for example, has called attention to four instrumental values that have been historically associated with justice—order, freedom, equality, and participation.[21] While Henry applies these norms within a domestic political context, they are also applicable to world politics as well.

If justice is to be promoted among states, it can only be done so if there is international order (peace). In domestic politics, order is ultimately guaranteed by sovereign states, each of which holds a monopoly of power in a particular territory. In world politics, by contrast, there is no sovereign power and therefore no ultimate guarantor of peace. In such an anarchic world system, order can be achieved only

---

[21] Paul Henry, *Politics for Evangelicals* (Valley Forge: Judson, 1974), pp. 82–84.

through the voluntary reform of nations, supported by a system of countervailing power among states.

The application of the three other instrumental values—freedom, equality, and participation—to world affairs presents more difficulties, because the aim of justice is the welfare of individuals, not states. Since these three norms directly affect the well-being of persons within political communities, it is essential to promote such values. But there is no similar compelling need to apply freedom, equality, and participation to the behavior of states. States are, of course, important in meeting human needs and maintaining social order, but they do not enjoy a status of moral equivalence with individuals.

The problems raised by equating the morality of states with the morality of individuals can be further illuminated if we distinguish between two different conceptions of justice. The first, *international justice,* concerns equity among states. Such a norm focuses on the morality of interstate behavior, giving special attention to the duties and rights of states. The moral norms in international justice include such rights as self-preservation and sovereign equality and the duty of nonintervention. To achieve this type of justice it is essential to preserve the integrity of each nation and to promote harmony among member states, but a stable world system in which each of the 160 states respects the others' territorial integrity need not be just, for there may be extreme poverty or political oppression within some states.

If Christians are to have a more comprehensive grasp of the morality of world affairs, it is important to supplement the first approach with another one. This second type of justice, called *world* or *cosmopolitan* justice, is concerned not with the morality of states per se, but with the morality of the world system. It focuses on people and on the international system and bypasses the state altogether. It assumes that the only way of promoting the common good of the world is through transnational institutions and the delimitations of state sovereignty. Whereas international justice attempts to work within the existing world system, cosmopolitan justice seeks to overcome the state-centric world. Although cosmopolitan justice is an idealistic and future-oriented conception, it is important because it defines morality in terms of people, not states.

Since cosmopolitan justice is concerned with the welfare

of people, its promotion will require all four instrumental values listed by Henry. Whereas international justice depends primarily on the value of order, the promotion of human rights and individual liberties will require the presence of freedom, political equality, and participation in the affairs of the world. Only when there is a high degree of pluralism can people begin to experience justice.

A PLURALISTIC STRATEGY

As noted previously, this study is based on a reformed theological perspective, or what Nicholas Wolterstorff has called "world-formative Christianity."[22] Such an approach assumes that God calls his people not to disengage from the problems and dilemmas of social and political life, but to seek to reform and transform the world. According to this perspective, the political institutions and social structures of the world are fallen. They are alienated from the will of the Creator. Rather than affirming justice, they have inhibited human dignity of people. The task of the Christian is therefore to promote reconciliation between God and people and to reform social structures in accordance with divine norms. The strategy is not to separate or to oppose; rather the aim is to redeem, infuse, and infiltrate all of society with God's love and righteousness. Since God uses his people to accomplish his tasks (e.g., missionaries are God's instruments of overseas evangelism), it is through sensitive, informed people that God's righteousness and justice can be brought to bear on world affairs.

If Evangelicals are to contribute to the task of political evangelism in world politics, they will need a strategy to direct their actions. Defining a strategy is especially important if the perils of a politicized faith are to be avoided. There are great dangers in speaking in the name of the Lord on world affairs issues. However, the difficulties and dangers should not lead men and women away from applying faith to the political realm, but should encourage a more authentic and faithful witness in the public arena. This will be possible only if Christians are guided by a strategy that is consistent with the Scriptures and responsible to the legitimate claims of national and transnational communities. At a minimum,

---

[22]Wolterstorff, Until Justice, p. 3.

such a strategy will be characterized by three traits—pluralism, competence, and charity.

Pluralism

Pluralism can be defined as the existence of a number of different competing views, each of which is considered legitimate. A defense of pluralism may appear, at first glance, as contrary to the Christian faith or, at the very least, as debilitating to an effective political strategy. Ideally, Christians should be united in matters of faith and practice. The church universal should be one large, cohesive community. But the unity of believers is an ideal, not a reality. We pray for the unity of the church, but there is division nonetheless. Why is there so much disagreement among Christians? Does not Christian discipleship depend on a belief in and practice of a simple faith? And if this is the case, ought not Christians to agree on the essential elements of political evangelism?

The problem, of course, is not faith itself, but our understanding and application of faith. Biblical faith is monistic; it is the one true religion. But God's truth is one thing; human apprehension and application is another. Because all human beings are sinful and finite, a pluralistic approach is the only approach that can be reconciled with the doctrine of sin. Christians need to affirm the gospel and the truth of the Scriptures, but their own understanding of that truth will always be tainted by their own frailty and sin. This is why a strategy of Christian political influence must be based on theistic pluralism—a Christian world view that tolerates different theological interpretations and practical expressions.

Historically, Christians have disagreed about the relationships of faith to human existence. H. Richard Niebuhr, in *Christ and Culture,* has identified five major approaches by which Christians have related faith to life, Christ to society. At one extreme are those who have viewed the kingdom of God and the temporal world as essentially complementary. At the other extreme are those who have viewed Christ and culture as fundamentally in opposition. And in between the extremes of "Christ of culture" and "Christ against culture" are three other approaches, including the reformed perspective adopted here, which views the kingdom of God and the world in continuing tension.[23] Given different theological presuppositions, it is unlikely that Christians will develop a cohesive strategy of political evangelism. Catholics, Baptists, Mennonites, and Presbyterians, for example, will disagree on the legitimacy of military force because they will hold different legitimate biblical interpretations on political resistance and war.

Another reason for public policy disagreement is that Christians will differ in their interpretation of problems and application of biblical and moral principles. Agreement with biblical principles does not automatically translate into public policy consensus. The principles of justice, righteousness, and love are absolute, yet their application by sinful persons—even those transformed by God's grace—is not. It is therefore unreasonable to expect public policy agreement among all those who seek to apply biblical truth to world affairs. The problem of applying biblical principles to public policy is well stated by Christian politician Stephen Monsma:

> If society were unitary in its needs and interests, finding the correct path to justice would be fairly simple. But seeking justice and correcting oppression involves parceling out advantages and disadvantages among contending forces, beliefs, and interests in society. It is seeking to give each its due in a situation of limited knowledge and time. In such a situation, to possess supreme confidence that one's own perspective on what is an equitable balance is correct and true is seldom, if ever, warranted. And surely to baptize one's own answers, even when carefully and prayerfully reached, as God's answers to man's dilemmas is untenable.[24]

Competence

A second major requirement of an effective strategy is skill and knowledge. Most problems of world politics are enormously complex, and the development of solutions is even more so. For example, human rights are violated throughout the world, and if the United States is to be a moral force in world affairs, it should help promote such rights. But underlying this simplistic affirmation lurk difficult

[23]H. Richard Niebuhr, *Christ and Culture* (New York: Harper and Row, 1951), pp. 1–11.
[24]Stephen Monsma, *Pursuing Justice in A Sinful World* (Grand Rapids: Eerdmans, 1984), p. 17.

and profound concerns. The following questions identify some of these: Which human rights are fundamental, and which are not? Should the United States use its influence to promote rights everywhere or only where it is most feasible? Which regimes are more threatening to human rights— military governments or totalitarian communist regimes? Should the United States give military and economic assistance if a regime violates human rights? To what degree should the United States use its influence to bring about democracy? Questions such as these are of course difficult in the abstract; they are even more intractable when applied to specific U.S. foreign policy problem areas, such as South Africa, Chile, Nicaragua, and the Soviet Union.

If the political strategy of Christians is to be credible and responsible, those who seek to influence public policy must be informed about the issues. They must have knowledge and competence. This is of course most difficult, especially since changes and developments in the problems of world politics are continuous and time and resources are limited. As a college political science professor, I have many resources for staying abreast of world politics, yet staying informed in my area of specialization, international relations, is always a great challenge and a never-ending task.

Given the complexity of today's issues, it is essential for Christians concerned with foreign affairs to select a few issues and concentrate on them rather than on the entire domestic or international political arena. As in all areas of life, competence is developed through specialization, and this requires focusing attention on a limited number of issues.

One of the common errors Christians make is to use religion and moral symbols to justify political preferences. This error may be the result of a hasty and careless integration of faith and public policy, or, at worst, it may be the manipulation of faith for political ends. The use of religion as a palliative, however, will not only contribute to an irresponsible foreign policy, but may weaken and damage authentic faith. The aim of integrating faith and politics, of course, is not to legitimize political interests, but rather to guide and assess politics in the light of transcendent norms. One of the reasons why the U.S. Catholic bishops' pastoral letter on nuclear strategy was so influential and important was the competence with which the bishops carried out their task. One may disagree with the conclusions of the pastoral letter, but there can be no doubt that it represented an informed, competent study undertaken by a morally sensitive, searching group of people.

Let me illustrate a careless application of faith and foreign policy. In September 1977, while the U.S. Senate was debating the merits of the proposed Panama Canal treaty, a group of Christians from San José, Costa Rica, wrote an open letter to North Americans in support of the treaty.[25] The letter stressed that the United States should transfer the sovereignty of the canal to Panama because it was in accord with the Scriptures. The letter's signatories stated that three biblical passages were especially relevant to the proposed treaty: (1) the story of Naboth's vineyard (1 Kings 21), the parable of Nathan (2 Samuel 12), and the law regarding the Year of Jubilee (Leviticus 25). While I believe there were many moral and prudential reasons for supporting the treaty, I find it difficult to see how these passages relate specifically to the problem at hand.

Another error in the integration of faith and public policy is the oversimplification of issues. A common mistake is the fallacy of dichotomous thinking, which involves dividing problems and policy alternatives into mutually exclusive categories. The world is not comprised of good nations and evil nations, rich people and poor people, advocates of peace and defenders of war. Of course, a major spiritual battle is being waged between right and wrong, good and evil, but it is wrong to simplistically identify international relations with this underlying spiritual battle. President Reagan made this error in his address at the National Association of Evangelicals' 1983 annual meeting when he identified U.S.–U.S.S.R. tensions as a moral conflict.[26] The United States has been a beacon of hope for many, and the Soviet Union has been one of the most brutal,

[25] Rolando Mendoza et al., "Open Letter to North American Christians," San Jose, Costa Rica, Sept. 11, 1977.

[26] *Remarks of the President.* The president warned against calling the arms race a giant misunderstanding and removing ourselves "from the struggle between right and wrong and good and evil." He suggested that the Soviet Union was an "evil empire" and proclaimed that "any objective observer must hold a positive view of American history, a history that has been the story of hopes fulfilled and dreams made into reality. Especially in this century, America has kept alight the torch of freedom, not just for ourselves but for the millions of others around the world."

repressive regimes in human history. But, because sin is constant and universal, the United States should never assume that it is the sole or even primary embodiment of God's goodness. The identification of the spiritual struggle with U.S.–Soviet conflicts is thus not only an oversimplification of a problem, but a distortion of reality. Faith needs to be integrated into public policy, but it needs to be done with skill, competence, and knowledge.

Charity

Finally, an effective political strategy must be characterized by tentativeness and humility. Reinhold Niebuhr has called attention in his writings to the dangers of fanatical religious politics. His perceptive wisdom is captured in the following statement:

> The sorry annals of Christian fanaticism, of unholy religious hatreds, of sinful ambitions hiding behind the cloak of religious sanctity, of political power impulses compounded with pretensions of devotion to God, offer the most irrefutable proof of the error in every Christian doctrine and every interpretation of the Christian experience which claim that grace can remove the final contradiction between man and God. The sad experiences of Christian history show how human pride and spiritual arrogance rise to new heights precisely at the point where the claims of sanctity are made without due qualifications.[27]

Charity and humility are essential in the political witness of the church because Christians need tentativeness and humility lest their divergent theologies and political approaches inhibit the unity of the church. H. Richard Niebuhr has written that the repeated struggles of Christians to define conclusively the relationship of faith to society have not yielded a single Christian answer, but only "a series of typical answers which together, for faith, represent phases of the strategy of the militant church in the world." Niebuhr further observes that God's strategy is in his own mind, not in the minds of his disciples. "Christ's answer to the problem

---

[27] While my research notes indicate that this quote is by Reinhold Niebuhr, I have been unable to document its source.

of human culture is one thing; Christian answers are another."[28]

The U.S. bishops' pastoral letter on peace concludes with the admonition that Christians seeking to promote peace in a nuclear age should not appropriate the authority of the church to defend particular prudential judgments about national security policy. Rather the letter says, "They should always try to enlighten one another through honest discussion, preserving mutual charity and caring above all for the common good. . . . Not only conviction and commitment are needed in the church but also civility and charity."[29]

A Christian approach to public policy must stress unity on principles and tolerate diversity in application. The application of basic scriptural norms must be done with integrity and an open mind, recognizing that there are different ways of defining problems and applying God's truth to the exigencies and vagaries of life. Christians are called to redeem the fallen institutions and structures of society. Given the enormous problems in world affairs and the substantial economic, political, and military resources of the United States, American Christians have a special role and responsibility in promoting human dignity worldwide. But in carrying out this political mandate, we need to remember with the apostle Paul that among faith, hope, and love, the greatest attribute is love.

---

[28] Niebuhr, *Christ and Culture*, p. 2.
[29] U.S. Catholic Bishops, "The Challenge of Peace: God's Promise and Our Response," *Origins*, May 19, 1983, p. 3.

3

JUSTICE IN THE INTERNATIONAL SYSTEM

"We should not view national boundaries as having fundamental moral significance. Since boundaries are not coextensive with the scope of social cooperation, they do not mark the limits of social obligation."

Charles R. Beitz[1]

"It may be regarded as axiomatic that the less a community is held together by cohesive forces in the texture of its life the more must it be held together by power. This fact leads to the dismal conclusion that the international community lacking these inner cohesive forces, must find its first unity through coercive force to a larger degree than is compatible with the necessities of justice. Order will have to be purchased at the price of justice."

Reinhold Niebuhr[2]

I have suggested that Christian discipleship involves the promotion of public justice and that promoting justice in the international system is difficult because of the absence of a common political authority and the lack of agreement among nations about the definition and application of justice. In this

---

[1]Charles R. Beitz, *Political Theory and International Relations* (Princeton: Princeton University Press, 1979), p. 151.

[2]Reinhold Niebuhr, *The Children of Light and the Children of Darkness* (New York: Scribner, 1960), p. 168.

chapter I shall further clarify the concept of justice as it relates to world politics and shall explore how Christians might contribute to a more just world order.

One of the major themes of this chapter is that the contemporary world system, notwithstanding its major problems, provides a morally acceptable framework of action, especially when considering proposed alternatives. The existing system, however, does pose major impediments to the quest for a humane, just world community. In particular, the right of state sovereignty often conflicts with other moral claims. In view of the great dangers posed by the anarchic world system, I shall explore briefly two special moral problems raised by the quest for international justice— war and foreign intervention. While war and military intervention are evil in that they violate moral rights of states, such actions may be legitimate under conditions of extreme emergency. If justice is to be an absolute norm, state sovereignty must occasionally be compromised in the service of the common world good.

APPROACHES TO INTERNATIONAL JUSTICE

I noted in the previous chapter that there are two definitions of justice—*international justice* and *world justice.* The first type of justice concerns the justice among states. It assumes that the existing world order of nation states is legitimate and that state boundaries are morally significant. The quest for justice is carried out internationally primarily through the actions of states. International justice will not guarantee justice within states, but it will promote the conditions that are essential for peace and harmony within the world. Without order there can be no justice among or within nations.

World justice, by contrast, is not concerned with justice among states, but with justice among peoples of the world. Its focus is the world as a single community. Its concern is the well-being of all the people of the world. Since the moral rights and duties of states derive from individuals, states are not themselves fundamental moral agents. A state is simply an instrumental community that serves the moral interests of people. The state was designed for people, not people for the state.

These two conceptions of justice have historically produced two approaches to morality and world affairs. The first approach, which Charles Beitz calls "the morality of states,"[3] emphasizes the existence of moral principles that are applicable to the behavior of states. It assumes that if states follow consistently and faithfully these norms in their interstate relations, international peace and justice will reign. Represented by writers such as Samuel Pufendorf, John Locke, John Stuart Mill, and recently by Michael Walzer,[4] this approach seeks to promote justice by working within the existing world system rather than by trying to transform it. The chief agents of international behavior are states, and world justice is promoted through their moral actions. Interstate or international justice is achieved among states through the actions and decisions of governments. Immoral behavior of states leads to injustice and occasionally to war.

To a significant degree, the moral principles that apply to the behavior of states are based on the rights and duties of individuals in a domestic political community. Just as individuals bear rights and responsibilities to one another within society, states must fulfill mutual obligations to other states within the world community. Among the most basic moral and legal rights enjoyed by states are those of political independence and territorial jurisdiction. The quest for international justice thus presupposes basic rights—namely, the rights of states to exist and to be politically independent. There can be no justice among states if the existence and political independence of states is jeopardized, but beyond the foundational rights of independence and territorial control, states have mutual moral obligations affecting commercial, political, and security interests. Hugo Grotius, for example, in *The Laws of War and Peace* delineated long ago various moral guidelines that states should follow in wartime. Building on historical precedent, natural law, and the Scriptures, Grotius argued that the behavior of states during war was subject to moral constraints. States were not free to do whatever they thought necessary for victory; rather they

---

[3] Charles R. Beitz, "Bounded Morality: Justice and the State in World Politics," *International Organization*, Summer 1979, p. 408.

[4] Michael Walzer, *Just and Unjust Wars* (New York: Basic Books, 1977); see also M. Walzer, "The Moral Standing of States: A Response to Four Critics," *Philosophy and Public Affairs*, vol. 9, no. 3 (Spring 1980), pp. 209–29, for a defense of the morality of states approach in the light of major criticisms against his book.

were to follow well-established moral principles governing the relations of hostile nations.

To be sure, states have not always behaved in accordance with such moral norms. This does not mean that relevant ethical standards do not exist, but only that the application of international morality is defined and applied subjectively by individual states. One of the distinctive features of international politics is the lack of moral consensus and, more importantly, public institutions by which the public good can be defined and implemented. Whereas in domestic society there is a common judge to interpret and enforce the law, in international society there is no such ultimate authority. As a result, implementation of justice is ultimately dependent on the initiatives of each state.

The alternative approach to justice is the world or cosmopolitan world view, represented by such thinkers as Francisco Suares, Emmanuel Kant, and contemporary writers such as Charles Beitz and Henry Shue.[5] Whereas the morality of states approach is concerned with the promotion of justice through the existing political framework, the cosmopolitan world view applies morality to individuals— indeed, to the peoples of all the world. According to Beitz, the world has become increasingly economically interdependent, and this has, in turn, resulted in a decline in state autonomy. He points out that because of growing international economic interdependence, the issues of distributive justice apply not only within states, but also among them. "Principles of distributive justice," writes Beitz, "must apply in the first instance to the world as a whole, and derivatively to nation-states."[6] Since individuals rather than states are the subjects of international morality, the cosmopolitan approach denies the moral significance of state boundaries and specifically of state sovereignty. Whereas sovereignty is a basic norm of the morality of states approach, the cosmopolitan view challenges the sovereignty of states and opens nations to external moral judgment.

Both the morality of states and cosmopolitan approaches provide useful frameworks for assessing world politics from a Christian world view. The morality of states, however, has

---

[5] Beitz, *Political Theory;* and Henry Shue, *Basic Rights* (Princeton: Princeton University Press, 1980).

[6] Beitz, *Political Theory*, p. 170.

the advantage of applying moral norms to the existing realities of world affairs. Its emphasis on the moral obligations of states provides a realistic approach to the development of a moral foreign policy without radically altering the structures of the world. The cosmopolitan approach is also useful in that it calls attention to the individual in the anarchic world order. Because all states differ in their abilities to meet human needs, many peoples in poor, repressive, totalitarian systems do not enjoy the dignity that is due them as human beings. But while individual needs must be of central concern to Christians, I believe it is unrealistic and unwise to radically shift attention from the state to the individual. If this study were concerned with the policies and actions of individuals and private associations, the cosmopolitan approach would obviously be most appropriate. However, since my concern here is chiefly with the public actions of governments and specifically with the making and implementation of U.S. foreign policy, I shall rely on the morality of states approach. Such a framework has the advantage of applying appropriate moral norms to the conduct of states. My assessment of international and world justice is therefore based on this perspective.

WORLD JUSTICE

Features of the World System

Our moral assessment of the existing international system must begin with a brief description of some of the key features. First, the world is divided into some 160 nation states, each claiming to be free and independent. This freedom and independence is denoted by the doctrine of sovereignty, which means that each state has ultimate authority within its national territory. The right of national independence is protected in the international system by the correlative duty to avoid intervention in the domestic affairs of other states. This is why sovereignty and nonintervention are complementary elements of the existing international legal order.

Second, since states are sovereign, there is no competent authority to settle disputes or to regulate the distribution of resources in the world. There are numerous governmental and nongovernmental institutions that facilitate international cooperation, but none can claim authority over the state. As a result, analysis of conflict resolution and distributive justice ultimately depends on the cooperative actions of states.

Third, the world is highly inegalitarian. States differ enormously in their size, wealth, and influence. Some states are large, others are small; some are rich, others are poor; some are richly endowed with primary resources, others are not; some have favorable topographies, others do not; some are strategically located for military and economic purposes, others are not. Clearly, the existing world system is a place of great inequalities. Some of these are a result of original conditions at the birth of states, while others are a consequence of different patterns of development and historical evolution. Since the world system is anarchical, the promotion and protection of national welfare is dependent chiefly on the efforts and initiatives of the people of each nation. This is why states seek to maximize their military, political, and economic capabilities and why the results of such efforts are so unequal.

Limitations

There are, of course, many problems and limitations with a decentralized, anarchic system of numerous competing autonomous states. Perhaps the most significant problem is war—a condition of hostilities between two or more countries. War is a direct by-product of the lack of an authoritative mechanism for peacefully settling disputes. Since there are no effective conflict-resolution institutions in the world, states resort to war to protect vital interests.[7] Another problem is international economic injustice—generally defined in terms of international economic inequalities. Although the problem is defined in terms of the egregious differences in average incomes among states, the moral urgency of this problem derives from the rampant and appalling poverty in the Third World.

Given the problems of war and international economic injustice, some people have concluded that the existing world system is morally unacceptable and that the only alternative is to abolish the existing system and construct a

[7]Quincy Wright once estimated that there had been an average of about one war every two years since the end of the fifteenth century—or roughly 278 wars. See his classic study, *On War* (Chicago: University of Chicago Press, 1942).

new world order. We can, of course, agree that the existing international order is not fully compatible with God's justice. Since sin is total and universal, all domestic and international structures are fallen, including the existing international political and economic structures. But having affirmed the fallenness of the contemporary international organizations, I know of no morally compelling argument that has been advanced for the abolition of the existing anarchic international system. The rules and institutions of the international system do not conform with God's standards of justice, to be sure, but they are not incompatible with the Scriptures or with accepted legal and moral principles. They do provide a useful, if imperfect, environment in which states can promote legitimate national and international interests.

The Legitimacy of States

To further appreciate the legitimacy of the state, it may be helpful to compare the state to smaller, more widely accepted human communities.[8] To some extent, countries are like neighborhoods, colleges, and families. They are like neighborhoods in that national cohesion depends significantly on common cultural, social, and ethnic features. Just as neighborhood unity results from shared cultural and social values and customs, national cohesion derives significantly from shared norms and aspirations, which together result in nationalism.

States are like colleges in that they seek to regulate membership. Whereas neighborhoods generally do not admit or exclude members, a feature of colleges is that they regulate admissions in accordance with stated aims and purposes. Admissions policies can be highly inegalitarian, of course, in that they may exclude many worthy applicants. But admissions policies, like the immigration laws of a state, are a significant feature of community life because they contribute to the formation and maintenance of cohesion and a sense of shared purpose. Just as an "open" admissions policy can lead to weak academic institutions, an open immigration policy will significantly weaken the common bonds of countries.

---

[8]I am indebted to Michael Walzer's insightful comparisons of the state and other more proximate human institutions. See his chapter "The Distribution of Membership" in *Boundaries: National Autonomy and Its Limits*, eds. Peter G. Brown and Henry Shue (Rowen & Littlefield, 1981).

Finally, states are like families in that they can assist people in need. While family commitments are generally directed toward next of kin, families can also provide care for friends and even occasionally for strangers in need. When the United States welcomed Vietnamese refugees after the fall of the Saigon government, it was responding to immediate human needs by modifying its traditional refugee immigration policies. Thus, states, like families, can serve as a place of refuge.

States have been compared to neighborhoods, colleges, and families in order to affirm, by analogy, their important role in human life. People find meaning in the context of human associations, whether at work, at home, or in the neighborhood. But they also derive meaning and purpose through identification with a nation. Like other more proximate human communities, states serve a legitimate function in organizing communal life. They provide geographical boundaries and the political structure in which social and economic life can flourish. To be sure, states can impede the development of concern for people of other states. Excessive nationalism has been a major source of evil in the world, but the solution does not lie in the abolition of the existing world system any more than the solution to economic exploitation lies in the elimination of private property.

There is, of course, a world community to which all human beings belong. But this community differs from the state and other more proximate communities in that it is held together by weak, slender affinities. The strength of community life is directly proportionate to the sense of shared values and goals. The weakness of the international community is not solely or even primarily due to the absence of clear territorial boundaries or recognized political authorities. Rather it derives from the absence of shared purposes and the lack of clearly identifiable community duties and obligations. The weakness of universal bonds and affinities does not mean, however, that there are no universal shared commitments and that people have no moral obligations beyond their state. It suggests instead that human beings bear a number of community affinities, some stronger than others, and that for the time being the commitments to local and national politics tend to be stronger than those toward the international system. Since the problems of war, international economic exploitation, and excessive national competition can only be reduced if world consciousness becomes stronger, the promotion of world affinities and obligations is a legitimate moral enterprise. Increasing public pressure against unwarranted and excessive nationalism can contribute toward a more cooperative, peaceful world.

In order to defend the existing anarchic system, I shall briefly examine two proposed world system alternatives. One of them is political, and the other is economic. The political proposal involves the radical transformation of world politics; the economic proposal involves the reform of the international economic practices and institutions. Whether or not systemic justice would be promoted by alternatives such as these depends on the merit of the proposals. Winston Churchill once commented that democracy was an evil system but was better than any other alternative. Thus, in assessing the morality of the existing political and economic order, we need to evaluate the legitimacy of the existing rules and institutions in terms of alternatives, not ideal or philosophic conceptions of justice.

An Alternative Political World System

The most common political proposal involves the creation of a world government in order to abolish the problem of war.[9] Those who advocate the shifting of power toward a single world government generally support a federal world state patterned after the American constitutional system. Following the social contract models of Thomas Hobbes and John Locke, world federalists assume that the problem of international violence is a result of too much freedom and that what is needed is a transfer of authority from the states to a central government. They believe that if nations could transfer ultimate authority to a central power, as states did in the United States in the late eighteenth century, the world would become far more peaceful and just.

Aside from the insuperable difficulties in implementing a new world order, there are two important shortcomings in

---

[9]There are numerous proposals for world government. For examples, see *A Constitution for the World* (Santa Barbara: Center for the Study of Democratic Institutions, 1965); and Greenville Clark and Louis B. Sohn, *World Peace Through World Law*, 3d ed., enlarged (Cambridge: Harvard University Press, 1966). For a criticism of such proposals see Reinhold Niebuhr, "The Illusion of World Government," in his *Christian Realism and Political Problems* (New York: Scribner, 1953), pp. 15–31.

world federalism. First, such a model erroneously assumes that community life is primarily the result of political and constitutional arrangements, that centralization of military force creates community. To be sure, a central political authority is indispensable in making and implementing rules for managing community discord; but the development of communities is inescapably related to a people's common geography, language, culture, ethnic background, and history. Sovereignty is an essential element of community life, but it is not the sole or even primary norm. Reinhold Niebuhr has observed, "government may be the head of the body . . . but it is not possible for a head to create a body."[10] The primary barriers to a world government are thus social and cultural, not just political. If a world community is to be developed, the voluntary habits of communication and cooperation among peoples of different nations must be significantly strengthened.

Second, world federalism overlooks the problems that could result from the centralization of political authority. James Madison, the father of the U.S. Constitution, once observed that the problem in establishing legitimate governments was to make them strong enough to control the people but sufficiently weak to control themselves.[11] While the centralization of political authority can contribute to the potential elimination of war, it can also result in another problem—totalitarianism. The challenge posed by international political reform is to establish a responsible central government—one strong enough to successfully resolve interstate conflicts peacefully but one also sensitive to human rights. The record of twentieth-century governments suggests that the misuse of power may pose as great a danger to civilization as the threat of war. Eliminating pluralism and constitutionalism would be a heavy price to pay for the prospect of greater international order. There is, therefore, no morally compelling justification for adopting a radical transformation in world politics.

But the moral justification for the existing international political system need not rest on the potential problems of world government. The nation-state system itself, notwith-

---

[10]Niebuhr, *Children*, p. 165.
[11]James Madison, *The Federalist Papers*, no. 51 (New York: New American Library, 1961), p. 322.

standing its enormous imperfections, is an acceptable framework in which states can fulfill their moral obligations in promoting justice. One of the major advantages of the nation-state system is that it permits a high degree of differentiation. A world of cultural and social uniformities would be a dull place indeed. An anarchic political order not only protects different cultures, but promotes social, political, and economic diversity—a diversity which leads to a less cohesive but more dynamic international system. A comparison between a totalitarian state and a constitutional, democratic country illustrates the advantages of a differentiated world community. Whereas a totalitarian regime like Cuba or China enjoys a high degree of order and consensus, it achieves this order at an unacceptable price—namely, the government regulation of significant aspects of human life. Democratic, pluralistic states like Italy or the Netherlands, by contrast, are far more conflictual and disorderly because their governmental institutions and political rules do not inhibit conflict and dissent as in closed societies. Moreover, while decision making is far less efficient in such regimes, they tend to enjoy far greater creative and productive energy. The anarchic world system, like a democratic, pluralistic regime, is thus based on the legitimacy of multiple political communities and distinct social and cultural patterns. The task of international politics is not to eliminate social and political diversity but to strengthen the forces of accommodation and reconciliation.

An Alternative Economic World System

Proposals for transforming the existing international economic order are based on the belief that the existing system of rules, practices, and institutions is unjust. It is alleged that it is unjust because it exploits the poor nations and is a major source of poverty in the Third World. The principal alternative international economic system which has been proposed is the New International Economic Order (NIEO).[12] Proponents of the NIEO proposal believe that the

[12] Another alternative economic reform is the Basic Human Needs (BHN) program. This reform proposal, based on the cosmopolitan approach to international morality, focuses on human dignity and justice, not on states' rights or justice among states. Fundamentally, this proposal does not seek to restructure the international system, but to create an alternative approach to economic development. The basic goal of the program is to reduce poverty

existing formal and informal international economic rules are responsible for world poverty and international economic injustice. According to them, the contemporary economic system favors the rich, powerful states of the North and exploits the weaker nations of the South.

While there have been many specific charges as to how the current system harms the developing nations, the fundamental demands of the NIEO are: (1) the need for large transfers of resources and technology from the rich nations to the poor nations, (2) the need for favorable treatment of the Third World nations in order to promote their economic expansion, and (3) the need to alter the machinery of international economic relations so that the poor nations are given greater participation and influence in international decision-making institutions.[13] The rationale for these claims is that the current distribution of economic resources is unjust—a conclusion based almost wholly on the highly unequal distribution in national per capita income.

Just as world government is not a satisfactory solution to the problem of limited order in the international system, the NIEO is not a satisfactory solution to the problem of

---

by expanding culturally appropriate employment opportunities at the local community level. Unlike the NIEO, it does not seek to transform the international economic order, but rather to transform the values and attitudes impeding the reduction of Third World poverty. A central concept of the BHN is its redefinition of development in human terms. Whereas development is generally associated with national economic expansion, the BHN proposal views growth not as an end in itself, but as a means of fulfilling basic human needs, including sufficient food, shelter, clothing, health, and education through self-help projects, community development, labor-intensive programs, and the expansion of rural projects. For a further discussion of the BHN proposal, see Samuel S. Kim, *The Quest for a Just World Order* (Boulder: Westview, 1984), pp. 166–70.

[13] The following are some of the principal NIEO proposals: (1) establishing commodity agreements for goods from developing nations; (2) increasing official development aid from the rich nations to the poor nations; (3) renegotiating the principles for allocating Special Drawing Rights (SDRs) by the International Monetary Fund (IMF) so that the developing nations get a larger share; (4) giving debt relief to the poor nations, either by forgiving or postponing repayment; (5) giving preferential treatment to LDC exports; (6) increasing transfer of appropriate technology to the Third World; (7) assuring the right of expropriation without regard to international legal conventions; and (8) altering decision-making procedures of the IMF and the World Bank to give greater influence to the Third World in those institutions.

international economic injustice. There may be moral reasons for reforming the existing international economic system in accord with principles of the NIEO. It may be desirable, for example, to decrease the level of income disparities among states through direct transfers or to establish other institutions to assist nations suffering from inflation and unemployment. The appeal of the NIEO, however, has resulted primarily from the assumption that such a reform would strengthen international economic justice—that is, it would improve the plight of the poor. The NIEO is not a proposal for eradicating Third World poverty, rather it seeks to redistribute economic power and resources among states.

Reducing political and economic inequalities among states is difficult because the existing decentralized system itself perpetuates inequities. As political scientist Robert Tucker has observed, world economic inequality is an inescapable outcome of a world system based on national sovereignty and territorial independence. To affirm the right of independence is to affirm the potential of economic disparities.[14] Such inequalities are, of course, not fixed in perpetuity but can be changed through the initiatives of individual states and through the collective reforms. But if changes are made through transnational institutions, they will inevitably lead to a delimitation of state autonomy.

The major shortcoming of the NIEO is that it focuses on the poverty of states, not the poverty of people. Reduction in international inequalities would not necessarily result in the reduction of Third World poverty. Indeed, since the major barriers to improved living conditions in the developing nations are the repressive regimes themselves, reducing Third World poverty will be realized only when national economic inequalities are diminished. Income differences between the rich nations and poor nations are of course significant. In 1982, for example, the average per capita income of the richest fifty-two states ($9,364) was more than thirty times the average personal income of the poorest forty states ($276). But however unequal interstate incomes may be, their moral unacceptability derives not from the rights of states per se, but from the rights of people. This is why political scientist Samuel Kim has observed that "interstate

---

[14]For a defense of international political and economic inequalities see Robert W. Tucker, *The Inequality of Nations* (New York: Basic Books, 1977).

justice, unless translated into human justice, is a legal abstraction devoid of moral weight."[15]

The contemporary world economic order is a relatively neutral framework. It rewards nations and peoples who are efficient in production and marketing. Regrettably, there is no international welfare fund to care for those nations and peoples who, for whatever reason, are comparatively unproductive. Some of the explanations that have been given for the low level of Third World productivity include: limited natural resources, exploitative foreign investment, unjust trading practices, and economic imperialism by the rich nations. I believe with P. T. Bauer and B. W. Yamey that the economic prosperity of the North is not the result of abundant resources, access to ample capital, or favorable terms of trade, but of the productive capacities of people. The foundation of wealth, they argue, lies in human qualities—"the aptitudes, social customs, motivations, modes of thought, social institutions and political arrangements."[16] It is these qualities, they note, that explain the people's willingness to work, save, take risks, and seek the investment opportunities resulting in economic growth. The rules and institutions of the world economy, in short, do not explain either the poverty or wealth of nations. They do, however, provide a neutral framework in which productive efforts are rewarded.

Our brief examination of political and economic alternatives suggests that, notwithstanding the imperfections of the existing world system, there is no morally superior alternative to the existing structures. The contemporary world order is an imperfect yet morally acceptable order. Christians can, and should, promote systemic justice, but this can be done most effectively not through the radical transformation of the existing order, but by refining and reforming the existing international framework.

Some developments that would strengthen systemic justice include: (1) decreasing trade barriers and promoting greater economic freedom within states; (2) increasing freedom of international travel and promoting international exchange of ideas in order to strengthen crosscultural

---

[15] Kim, *Quest*, p. 165.
[16] P. T. Bauer and B. S. Yamey, "Against the New Economic Order," *Commentary*, April 1977, p. 28.

communication and understanding; (3) strengthening of international law by expanding the scope of the law in areas of common international concern (e.g., the sea and space) and by increasing respect for the international legal institutions, such as the World Court in The Hague or the European Court of Justice; (4) strengthening of international control of nuclear technology by increasing the number of signatory states to the Non-Proliferation Treaty (there are about thirty nonsignatories), encouraging stricter compliance with its provisions, and strengthening the International Atomic Energy Agency, a United Nations body responsible for monitoring nuclear power facilities; (5) expanding the political and economic role of regional and international organizations, especially the United Nations; (6) strengthening governmental and nongovernmental organizations concerned with the worldwide promotion of human rights; and (7) promoting respect for the principle of nonintervention and the corollary right of self-determination. Since the international system is a relatively neutral framework, the promotion of justice will result not from institutional changes per se, but from the moral behavior of states, especially the actions of superpowers. Given the enormous political and military power of the United States and the Soviet Union, improving the existing world order will be possible only if the two superpowers can increase their level of shared values and commitment to the transnational values and institutions that promote and protect peace and justice.

Because God loves the world, Christians have a special obligation to defend the interests of all human beings. They can do this by directly responding to human needs, by promoting systemic justice, and by encouraging a foreign policy guided by a universal commitment to human dignity. At the same time, Christians must participate fully in the other communities to which they belong. The promotion of justice will thus require the balancing of multiple, and sometimes competing, commitments among numerous communities, including the heavenly kingdom, the world system, the nation, the church, the neighborhood, and the professional associations and interest groups in which people participate.

INTERNATIONAL JUSTICE

The primary agents for promoting justice in world politics are states. But states can be unjust. They can pursue evil policies, domestically and internationally. They can champion their own national interests in disregard for, or at the expense of, the rights and interests of other states. The moral problem in foreign affairs is to develop policies that support legitimate national interests without violating the just rights of other states. But there is another insuperable obstacle involved in promoting international justice. This is the problem of making foreign policy when two moral claims are in conflict. Since justice and nonintervention are not always complementary goals, the promotion of justice may require the qualification of state sovereignty. And since the violation of the sovereignty of states involves evil, the quest for justice will always be a morally ambiguous undertaking.

In order to illustrate the moral ambiguity of a foreign policy, I shall examine two specific moral problems—war and military intervention. Both problems are significant because they involve the qualification of states' rights in order to promote a higher moral good. Both involve exceptions to the right of national independence: first, states may go to war (that is, attack the territory of a foreign state) against states which have previously committed criminal aggression; second, states may violate the territorial sovereignty of other nations under conditions of national emergency. While there is much disagreement about what conditions of national emergency might justify intervention, extreme human rights violations along with a threat to regional security might justify a defensive military intervention.

The Justice of War

War is generally defined as the ultimate method by which international disputes are settled. War is always evil because it results in many civilian and military casualties and widespread destruction. But war is not always the only or most serious evil. The moral problem of war is therefore to define the conditions under which state violence may be used against another state.

One of the most helpful approaches to the moral problem of war is the just war doctrine, which has its roots in

Greek and Roman philosophy and in the teachings of the early and medieval Christian church. According to the just war doctrine, war is morally legitimate if it promotes justice. More specifically, war can be justified if it combats unjust aggression and is carried out in a just, moral manner. Nations are not content with the status quo, but seek continuously to increase their influence and resources. As a result, when states use force to expand their influence and control in the world or to rectify perceived injustices, they will inevitably commit aggression, violating a basic right of states.

Fundamentally, the just war doctrine provides the ethical norms for determining when a war can be waged (*jus ad bellum*) and the principles for determining how a war should be fought (*jus in bello*). According to the doctrine, before war can be considered moral, at least five conditions must be met:

1. The cause of war must be just. Specifically, the only legitimate cause for fighting is to stop aggression. Only aggression justifies the violence of war.
2. All peaceful means must be exhausted before resorting to war. War can be justified only when it is a last resort measure.
3. War must be directed by competent authority. Since war must serve only a public good, not the private interests of individuals, military force can only be used when a government has officially declared and prosecuted a war.
4. War must have limited objectives. These objectives must be proportional to the goal of a just peace.
5. War must have a high probability of success. The application of force must have a high degree of bringing about justice in a reasonable period of time at a reasonable cost. Unlimited wars are immoral.[17]

While all of these conditions are important, the first is the most fundamental. It is the most basic norm because the contemporary world system rests on the territorial and political rights of its member states—rights that can be

---

[17]For a comprehensive treatment of the just war doctrine, see Paul Ramsey, *The Just War: Force and Political Responsibility* (New York: Scribner, 1968).

enjoyed only if states respect each other's sovereignty. This is why the principle of nonintervention is one of the pillars of the present international system and a cornerstone of the United Nations. The U.N. charter affirms this principle in article 2.4: "All members shall refrain in their international relations from the threat or use of force against the territorial integrity or political independence of any other state. . . ." The Organization of American States, of which the United States is a member, similarly calls on states to stop direct and indirect interference in the internal affairs of other states.[18] Given the legal and moral sanctity of nonintervention, it is not surprising that the failure to abide by this norm can result in disastrous consequences—for the victim as well as the aggressor. Respect for state sovereignty is basic. This is why the threat or use of force against another state can justify a war of self-defense.

Michael Walzer in *Just and Unjust Wars* provides an especially illuminating account of the moral legitimacy of war in response to foreign aggression.[19] Following the just war doctrine, Walzer develops a theory of war based on the "domestic analogy"—a comparison of domestic political communities with the international system. According to him, states have rights in the international community just as individuals have rights in domestic society. Among these rights are territorial independence and political sovereignty, and their violation by another state is a criminal act. According to Walzer, any use or imminent threat of military force by one state against another constitutes aggression and justifies forceful resistance and eventual punishment carried out either by the victim or by other states or both. The only justification for resorting to war is for defensive purposes—to protect legitimate national interests from foreign aggression.

For Walzer, the existing international system of independent and free states is moral. States are morally bound to respect each other's sovereignty by not interfering or intervening in the internal affairs of other states. But in order to protect the sovereignty of states, Walzer, following the just

---

[18]Article 18 of the charter of the Organization of American States says, "No State or group of States has the right to intervene, directly or indirectly, for any reason whatever, in the internal or external affairs of any other State."

[19]Walzer, *Just Wars*, ch. 4.

war doctrine, affirms the right to defend with force legitimate national interests. Since self-defense and nonintervention are not morally equivalent terms, the right of defense always takes precedence over the duty of nonintervention. States not only have the right of self-defense—a right affirmed by article 51 of the U.N. charter—but the responsibility to help protect other nations from foreign aggression. Nonintervention is a foundational norm of the existing international system, but it cannot serve as a shield for protecting criminal behavior. In short, the rule of nonintervention may be violated to protect legitimate interests.

The existing international political order provides a morally adequate system in which to carry out God's justice, but the pursuit of justice is possible only if states recognize each other's rights and live peacefully and harmoniously with each other. Just as individuals are prone to violate the rights of others, states are prone to commit aggression against the territorial sovereignty of other states. And since there is no central authority to protect states from criminal behavior in the world system, they must rely on their own military power to protect legitimate national interests. The purpose for military power is not to promote the extension of influence and control, but only to defend national and allied interests from external threats. There can be no moral justification for expansionistic and imperialistic wars, no matter how moral they may be. Failure to recognize the legitimacy of other states' rights will result in the complete destruction of the existing world system.

Military Intervention

Military intervention involves the sending of military forces either to provide military support to a regime threatened by rebel insurgency or to help defeat the ruling authorities who have committed grossly immoral and unjust policies. Military intervention is a much more significant violation of the rule of nonintervention than rescue operations (such as the Entebbe airport raid of 1976) or single bombing attacks (such as the Israeli destruction of the Baghdad nuclear reactor in 1983 or the destruction of the PLO headquarters in Tripoli in 1985). It is more serious because it involves the direct placement of foreign military forces which qualify the sovereignty of a state. Since intervention is the most extreme form of foreign interference (other forms include clandestine operations), it should be undertaken only as a last resort.

Military intervention, like war, is an illegal and immoral act—illegal because it violates the rule of nonintervention and immoral because it violates the principle of self-determination.[20] Violation of nonintervention may be justified in a few limited circumstances, but such action must always be taken under exceptional conditions and must be based on the presumption that intervention is generally wrong. The enforcement of justice may require the invasion of a state's sovereignty, but the circumstances must always be exceptional. It is important to stress the overarching principle of nonintervention because imperial powers have often violated states' rights simply to extend political influence in the world. But imperialism is not a legitimate justification for military intervention.

Nor is the advancement of democracy a sufficient justification for breaking the nonintervention norm. States need to be treated as self-determining entities in order to develop the institutions which best fit their history and culture. Walzer, following John Stuart Mill,[21] argues that state autonomy should not be violated in order to promote good government. "There are things that we cannot do for [other countries]," writes Walzer, "even for their own ostensible good."[22] Tyranny may be bad and democracy beneficial, but states must determine their own political practices and institutions. They must be allowed to struggle, for as Mill points out, only during an authentic struggle can people develop the virtues and practices required for the maintenance of a free society. Practicing self-determination runs the risk that some countries may not establish institutions that affirm and protect human dignity. Although we may wish that all societies would adopt the institutions and practices of representative, constitutional government, the decision as to what types of institutions must be decided by each nation.

Walzer recognizes that self-determination and the promotion of democracy may conflict, but he argues that state

---

[20]For a discussion of this point, see Hedly Bull, ed., *Intervention in World Politics* (Oxford: Clarendon, 1984).

[21]John Stuart Mill, "A Few Words on Non-Intervention," *Dissertations and Discussions*, vol. 3 (Boston: Wm. V. Spencer, 1868).

[22]Walzer, *Just Wars*, p. 89.

autonomy needs to be affirmed whether or not democratic institutions are likely to emerge. Political self-determination is important, he says, because it is more basic—"more inclusive"—than freedom and democracy, for it describes not only the particular political institutions of society, but the process by which a state arrives at a political arrangement. Walzer writes that "the members of a political community must seek their own freedom, just as the individual must cultivate his own virtue. They cannot be set free, as he cannot be made virtuous, by any external force."[23]

If intervention is to be legitimate, it must fulfill two conditions: first, it must be designed to counter grossly immoral and illegal acts; second, it must be strategically necessary. States can do evil to their own people and to the people of other nations. And when governments carry out actions that either threaten other states or result in massive enslavement and death of people, they lose their moral standing among states. President Theodore Roosevelt, in his annual message to Congress in December 1904, called attention to the limitations of the principle of political independence in the face of gross moral violations:

> We have plenty of sins of our own to war against, and under ordinary circumstances we can do more for the general uplifting of humanity by striving with heart and soul to put a stop to civil corruption, to brutal lawlessness and violent race prejudices here at home than by passing resolutions about wrong doing elsewhere. Nevertheless there are occasional crimes committed on so vast a scale and of such peculiar horror as to make us doubt whether it is not our manifest duty to endeavor at least to show our disapproval of the deed and our sympathy with those who have suffered by it. The cases must be extreme in which such a course is justifiable.[24]

Since nonintervention is not the highest moral rule of diplomacy, the promotion of justice may, under extraordinary circumstances, necessitate its violation.

But what is immoral behavior? What state actions constitute "gross immorality"? While scholars disagree on

[23] Ibid., p. 87.
[24] Quoted in Philip C. Jessup, "An Ethical Base for Foreign Policy," in Theodore M. Hesburgh and Louis J. Halle, *Foreign Policy and Morality: Framework for Moral Audit* (New York: CRIA, 1979), p. 49.

conditions that might justify intervention, there is widespread agreement that states should affirm human dignity domestically and promote peace internationally and that, when they fail to uphold such fundamental norms, they lose their moral standing among the community of states. When, for example, states threaten the basic human rights of a large portion of people through blatant massacre or enslavement or forced relocation, they violate fundamental standards of human dignity. This is why the Indian intervention in East Pakistan in 1971 was morally legitimate. As a result of the massive holocaust carried out by the Pakistani military forces against the Bengali people, India, which had accepted several million refugees fleeing the massacre, intervened and defeated the Pakistani military forces carrying out this inhuman action.

But if intervention is to be prudent and moral, it needs to be justified not solely in terms of morality, but also in terms of strategic necessity. Immorality per se is a necessary but insufficient condition for carrying out military intervention. Charles Krauthammer has pointed out, "To intervene solely for reasons of democratic morality is to confuse foreign policy with philanthropy. And a philanthropist gives out his own money. A statesman is a trustee."[25] If an action is to be considered strategically necessary, it must benefit directly the people on whose behalf intervention is carried out, and it must be essential to the long-term interests of the intervening state and its allies. Conflicts in the world are not random. The tensions between the United States and the Soviet Union, for example, have their root in a contest between two radically different world views. The contest between these two distinct ideologies is not limited to the direct bilateral relations of these two nations, however, but is expressed in the international politics of every region of the world. When the United States undertakes an action for strategic reasons, it does so because it enhances core democratic values in a conflict of vital and long-term importance.

The U.S. military intervention in Grenada in October 1983 illustrates the application of strategic necessity. The problem had its genesis in the forceful government takeover in 1979 by a group of revolutionary leaders of the New Jewel

---

[25]Charles Krauthammer, "When to Intervene," *The New Republic*, May 6, 1985, p. 11.

Movement, a Marxist-Leninist organization. After the 1979 coup, the ruling party quickly expanded its influence domestically and regionally, in large measure with Soviet, Cuban, and East European support. By 1983 Grenada had a Marxist-Leninist party, complete with central committee and politburo; an army and militia that outstripped the combined forces of all of its Caribbean neighbors; a well-developed propaganda machine relying on government-monopolized media and mass organizations; and an effective internal security apparatus to eliminate political opposition. The increasing military capabilities and revolutionary character of Grenada created an unstable and threatening regional environment.

The U.S. intervention was triggered by the breakdown of public order because of the murder of the prime minister, three cabinet ministers, and other political leaders. When civil unrest broke out, the governor general of the island (Sir Paul Scoon) requested outside assistance in restoring order. In addition, the Organization of Eastern Caribbean States—a seven-nation regional organization—formally requested the United States, along with Barbados and Jamaica, to restore public order. Finally, the breakdown of order posed a potential threat to the safety of approximately one thousand U.S. citizens on the island. While U.S. action was justified in order to protect U.S. lives and to respond to requested assistance, there was an additional unstated justification: Grenada had become a military threat to neighboring states and a vehicle for expanding Marxist-Leninist values in the region.[26] In the light of the breakdown of moral order and the strategic importance of the revolutionary developments in Grenada, there can be little doubt of the legitimacy of the United States' intervention.

In summary, I have argued that the pursuit of international justice may require the violation of state boundaries and involve, as a last resort, the use of force. Sovereignty

---

[26] That the Grenada intervention had broad strategic significance is suggested by such facts as: the primary military opposition to U.S. military action came from Cubans; nearly 200,000 tons of Soviet-bloc military equipment were captured after U.S. forces defeated the largely foreign garrison on the island; five secret military agreements with the Soviet Union, North Korea, and Cuba were discovered; and almost nine hundred Cuban, Soviet, North Korean, Libyan, East German, and Bulgarian personnel were expelled.

and territorial integrity are basic norms of the international political system, but they are not the sole, or even primary, ethical standards of the world. The protection of human dignity, political freedom, national security, domestic prosperity, and international peace are also legitimate moral norms. When tyrannical regimes undertake systematic oppression, and when imperialistic governments attempt to impose their will on others, they violate basic principles of the existing international system. The norm of nonintervention, however important, cannot and must not provide a shield for protecting immoral behavior of states.

The pursuit of moral foreign affairs must involve the discernment and application of multiple moral claims. The challenge in bringing ethical norms to bear on foreign policy is to illuminate the relevant standards and to then choose a policy among legitimate alternatives, recognizing that any action will bear some evil. I have suggested that foreign policy will be morally ambiguous precisely because it will involve choosing among moral alternatives. Whether war and military intervention are morally permissible, for example, cannot be ascertained in a vacuum but only in a specific historical context. The task of Christians is to clarify and defend relevant moral norms appropriate for the defense of liberty, security, peace, and prosperity and to apply them to the specific challenges of world and international justice.

4

PROMOTING PEACE AND PREVENTING ANNIHILATION

"Nothing is more disturbing or instructive than reading theologians twisting, wriggling and squirming when they face the problem of deterrence."

Stanley Hoffmann[1]

"One must currently choose between the unsatisfactory and the still more unsatisfactory. Anyone who thinks otherwise has not grasped the strange and desperate quality of our situation."

James Finn[2]

". . . unless one takes the two extreme positions of either unconditionally forbidding the use of force or pursuing self-interest without due regard to moral considerations . . . , one has inevitably embarked upon a course that will lead to questions of politics and strategy which have no simple or unambiguous answers."

Pierre Hassner[3]

---

[1] Stanley Hoffmann, *Duties Beyond Borders* (Syracuse: Syracuse University Press, 1981), p. 52.

[2] James Finn, "Nuclear Terror: Moral Paradox," *America*, Feb. 19, 1983, p. 129.

[3] Pierre Hassner, "Arms Control and Morality" in *Ethics, Deterrence and National Security*, Foreign Policy Report, June 1985 (New York: Pergamon-Brassey's, 1985), p. 33.

A key responsibility of Christians is to promote peace. This task has always been difficult and challenging, especially since Christians have historically held different theological perspectives on war. But the problem of peacekeeping in our generation has been radically transformed by science. The arrival of nuclear and thermonuclear weapons has transformed the Christian's peacekeeping mandate. Christians most now be concerned not only with the limitation of war, but also with ensuring that nuclear conflict never occurs.

The invention of nuclear and thermonuclear power has provided states with an unprecedented military potential, adding great urgency to the peacekeeping quest. This urgency is captured by Jonathan Schell, author of the widely publicized book, *The Fate of the Earth*, who writes: "Two paths lie before us. One leads to death, the other to life."[4] Because of the magnitude of destructive power of nuclear weapons, they are not easily encompassed in the traditional paradigms of world politics or in the traditional moral theories of war. Fundamentally, the application of nuclear physics has given states unimaginable destructive power by which to protect vital national interests but also by which to harm, if not destroy, themselves. Herein lies the nuclear dilemma: nuclear weapons are instruments of national defense, but they are also instruments of mass destruction and possibly even annihilation. The challenge is to identify and define an appropriate moral policy for these weapons.

Although the concern of this chapter is the promotion of peace, I shall examine only the dilemma posed by nuclear weapons. The challenge posed by nuclear arms is not, of course, the only problem in international peacekeeping, but it does illuminate in a stark manner the complexities and ambiguities involved in reconciling military force with justice. Moreover, the topic of nuclear morality has been much discussed and analyzed by churches and religious groups here and abroad as they have sought to influence the evolution of U.S. nuclear strategy. Indeed, during the early 1980s no other public policy issue received as much attention from American and Western European Christians as the problems of nuclear strategy and arms control.

---

[4]Jonathan Schell, *The Fate of the Earth* (New York: Avon Books, 1982), p. 231.

It is important to emphasize that peace in the nuclear age (commonly defined in terms of survival) is not the sole objective. If that were so, the peacemaking task would be much easier, as it would involve the search for harmony at all costs. If survival is the highest good, the only legitimate function of nuclear strategy is to inhibit war. States seek not only peace, however, but also the protection of vital interests. As Schell has observed, states deploy nuclear weapons not only to prevent nuclear aggression, but also to protect national sovereignty.

> People do not want deterrence for its own sake; indeed they hardly know what it is, and tend to shun the whole subject. They want the national sovereignty that deterrence promises to preserve. National sovereignty lies at the very core of the political issues that the peril of extinction forces upon us.[5]

Thus U.S. military defense—nuclear and conventional—serves not only to preserve peace, but also to inhibit aggression. For the Christian there is an additional claim: not only must nuclear weapons preserve peace and protect legitimate national interests, but they must also promote world justice. A morally satisfying approach to the nuclear dilemma must not only reduce the probability of war, especially nuclear war, but it must also promote the common good. There has been an increasing tendency among Christians to adopt the secularist peacekeeping agenda, which has placed survival as the highest moral good. But, as George Weigel has noted, such a value is contrary to the Christian church's teachings over the past two thousand years.[6] Christians are called to preserve the world and also to promote peace with justice. This is the distinctive contribution Christians should bring to world affairs.

The aim of this chapter is to examine how Christians, considering biblical norms, can contribute to peace and justice among states in the light of the specific challenge posed by nuclear weapons. First, I shall examine the problem of war and biblical perspectives on war. I shall then analyze the morality of nuclear strategy—focusing on the legitimacy of deterrence itself. Finally, I shall analyze two different

---

[5] Ibid., p. 217.

[6] George Weigel, "Open Letter to Archbishop Bernardin," *Catholicism in Crisis,* Jan. 1983, p. 15.

approaches for promoting peace and offer a number of specific policy recommendations which can reduce the chance of nuclear conflict.

THE PROBLEM OF WAR

The existence of nuclear weapons raises many profound moral questions: May states possess nuclear weapons, and if so, may they threaten their use? If threats are permissible, which types of threats are morally acceptable or preferable? Finally, if deterrence breaks down, may a state use nuclear arms? Because the possession of nuclear arms significantly enhances national power, states desire to possess nuclear arms. But nuclear weapons differ from conventional arms in that they do not provide "usable" force by which they can conquer and control foreign territories. Their chief legitimate purpose is to deter—to threaten punishment against states committing prior nuclear aggression. The moral dilemma of nuclear strategy is that deterrence is not self-validating. If deterrence is to be credible—that is, to effectively inhibit nuclear aggression—then superpowers need to make preparations for nuclear war. But preparations for carrying out nuclear retaliation can themselves increase the possibility and probability of nuclear conflict.

The destructive potential of nuclear weapons is enormous. The power of nuclear arms is generally measured by comparing their explosive force to the amount of TNT needed to create the same effect—usually a matter of thousands or millions of tons (kilotons and megatons). The Hiroshima bomb, for example, had a capacity of 12.5 kilotons. The warheads on modern land-based and sea-based missiles typically carry many times the destructive power of the earlier bombs, and the large hydrogen weapons carried by bombers can be from one thousand to two thousand times more powerful than the Hiroshima bomb. A single 25 megaton bomb would unleash greater energy than all the bombs dropped in Europe during the Second World War. It has been estimated that the two superpowers have more than fifty thousand nuclear warheads and that the destructive potential of these weapons exceeds 2.5 tons of TNT for every person in the world.

The danger of nuclear weapons also derives from the ease and quickness with which they can be delivered to their targets. The strategic nuclear weapons of the United States and the Soviet Union are based on three distinct legs known as the triad: intercontinental ballistic missiles (ICBMs), submarine-launched ballistic missiles (SLBMs), and bombers. During the past two decades major technological developments have been made in the nuclear arsenals of the two superpowers, but by far the most important innovations have involved the larger number of warheads carried per missile and the increasing accuracy of the delivery systems. Until the mid 1960s, missiles were capable of carrying only one warhead. Now the ICBMs and SLBMs carry numerous warheads, each of them targeted independently. Thus one Trident submarine can carry twenty-four missiles, each carrying from ten to fourteen separate nuclear warheads. Missiles too have become much more accurate, with the result that they now pose a threat to each other's fixed land-based missiles and bombers. Indeed, the increasing potential vulnerability of the American ICBM strategic nuclear forces has been responsible for much of the U.S. debate about nuclear strategy during the 1980s.

The threat of nuclear conflict is rooted in the problems of an anarchic international system where 160 states compete for scarce resources and where no authoritative supranational institutions exist for resolving disputes. Because each state must rely on its own resources to protect its legitimate interests, states seek to maximize power, especially military power. Moreover, because there is no final arbiter to settle disputes, war has historically been the ultimate instrument of conflict resolution in world affairs.[7] While the threat of war looms over all civilization, the application of nuclear technology to armaments has radically changed the nature of warfare. In the light of the destructive potential of nuclear

---

[7]Quincy Wright, who has written the definitive study of war (*A Study of War*) found that from the end of the fifteenth century to the mid twentieth century there had been 278 wars—or roughly about one war every two years. This century has experienced two of the most destructive wars of all time, involving more than 90 million deaths. Fortunately, since 1945 there have been no direct wars between the two superpowers, although there have been numerous regional conflicts in which they have been involved indirectly. Moreover, since 1945 Third World nations have been involved in many conventional wars, resulting in more than 11 million deaths. The war between Iran and Iraq of the early 1980s alone has resulted in nearly a million deaths.

and thermonuclear weapons, the challenge now is not only to keep the peace, but to preserve the universe.

Ideally, the world would be safer had nuclear fission and fusion never been harnessed. But the technology exists, and the weapons are here. Even if diplomats could negotiate multilateral nuclear disarmament agreements, there would always be the possibility of nuclear blackmail. A sound peacekeeping strategy must therefore be based on the reality that nuclear power cannot be wished away. Like all power, nuclear power will have to be managed, and the dominant moral issue in U.S. foreign policy in the contemporary age is to devise a strategy that both protects liberty and justice and inhibits war.

Deterrence

Deterrence has been the fundamental postulate of U.S. nuclear strategy during the postwar decades. As worked out originally in the early 1950s, the basic aim of American nuclear weapons is deterrence—the prevention of major aggression against the United States and its allies by implicitly threatening retaliation. The notion of preventing harm through punishment or the threat of punishment is, of course, not an invention of the nuclear age, but one that is almost as old as civilization itself. But the application of this idea to nuclear weapons has given it a completely new meaning. Whereas the failure of conventional deterrence results in limited punishment, the failure of nuclear deterrence leads to mass destruction. It is this threat of nuclear holocaust that has maintained a balance of terror—a balance where each superpower faces the other, knowing that failure to keep peace will lead to mass destruction in both societies. Winston Churchill aptly described this condition in a speech in the House of Commons in 1955: "Safety will be the sturdy child of terror, and survival the twin brother of annihilation."[8]

The condition of assured destruction is similar to a circus where two fencers are on a tightrope threatening each other. Each fencer carries a sword and explosives tied around his waist that will explode and kill everyone in the circus if he falls. Each fencer threatens the other in the game of fencing, knowing that his own interest is maximized by ensuring a

---

[8]Quoted in Schell, *Fate of the Earth,* p. 197.

stalemate. Each fencer knows that victory will also mean defeat, for the defeat of the fencer would result in his fall from the high wire and lead to the destruction of both fencers and observers. The game of fencing thus continues with the hope that neither player will tire, lose his footing, or undertake an action that would destroy his opponent. In this game neither party can win, although both could lose. The problem is to find a way to terminate the game without anyone getting hurt, but nobody has been able to do that yet.

The continued modernization of strategic nuclear arms has not altered the fundamental "game" of deterrence, although it has introduced changes that make it more delicate and precarious. Rational, moral persons have not been able to solve the predicament posed by the condition of assured destruction. The basic problem facing the Christian peacemaker is whether to accept and support this strategy in which evil (massive destruction) is threatened in order to achieve good (peace and justice). If this strategy is morally unacceptable, as pacifists proclaim, then Christians bear a moral responsibility to support unilateral nuclear disarmament or a variant of such a position. If nuclear deterrence, on the other hand, is not the supreme evil, but is an evil that must be temporarily tolerated for greater goods—world peace and protection from totalitarian communist aggression—then the task of Christians must be to strengthen deterrence and ensure that every measure is taken to inhibit the use of nuclear weapons.

BIBLICAL AND THEOLOGICAL PERSPECTIVES ON PEACEMAKING

Biblical Perspectives

One of the biblical principles of great significance is the ideal of peace. While human sin has brought war and injustice, the eternal ideal of *shalom* challenges all Christians to participate in the making of a more harmonious, peaceful world.

The biblical mandate for peace is supported in both the Old and New Testaments. The sixth commandment of the Decalogue says, "You shall not murder" (Exod. 20:13). And while God commanded Israel to go to war repeatedly to root out the evil of other nations, the hope for peace was expressed continually. Similarly, the people of Israel were encouraged to pray for the peace of Jerusalem (Ps. 122:6). And because King David was regarded as a man of war, he was denied his dream of building a temple for Jehovah (1 Chron. 22:8–9). The prophets also repeatedly articulated the yearning for peace. Isaiah described the hope of peace when God will stand as the judge of nations:

> They will beat their swords into plowshares
> and their spears into pruning hooks.
> Nation will not take up sword against nation,
> nor will they train for war anymore.

(Isa. 2:4)

The prophet Micah also longed for peace and repeated the promise about the day when men shall learn war no more (Mic. 4:3).

While the New Testament includes fewer references to peace than the Old Testament, it provides much more guidance to the personal qualities that lead to interpersonal and international harmony. Jesus declared in his Sermon on the Mount: "Blessed are the peacemakers" (Matt. 5:9). The Gospels repeatedly record the importance of love in human relationships. In John we read Jesus' love command: "A new command I give you: Love one another. As I have loved you, so you must love one another" (13:34). The apostle Paul says that one of the attributes of Christian conduct is never to repay evil with evil and never to get revenge. Rather evil should be conquered with good (Rom. 12:14–21).

Theological Perspectives

While the call to peacemaking is clear in the Scriptures, Christians have been deeply divided about whether and how military force should be used in settling disputes.[9] Some have been of the view that war can be an instrument of righteousness and justice. This approach, known as the crusade, is based on the conviction that just as God used Israel to punish evil, God can use states to pursue his will in the contemporary world. According to crusaders, military

---

[9]For an excellent short comparison of different Christian perspectives on war see Robert G. Clouse, ed., *War: Four Christian Views* (Downers Grove: InterVarsity, 1981). A more comprehensive account is Roland H. Bainton, *Christian Attitudes Toward War and Peace; a Historical Survey* (Nashville: Abingdon, 1960).

power is legitimized by the goals. At the opposite extreme are the pacifists who believe that violence is inconsistent with the demands of the kingdom of God. According to them, Jesus calls us to a radical lifestyle involving love, meekness, and nonviolence. Since the use or threat of violence is wrong, Christian pacifists oppose all aspects of nuclear strategy. They oppose the possession, threat, and use of nuclear weapons. For them, the issues of national security policy are clear and simple: Do not rely on conventional or nuclear military power.

In between these two perspectives is the just war doctrine. According to this approach, the possession and use of military power are morally legitimate provided their goals and means are just. While all war is evil, some wars may be just, provided they meet certain criteria, such as: the cause must be just; the use of violence must be a last resort; the objectives of war must be limited; there must be a high probability of success; and finally, the use of force must be carried out in a just way. This last principle has historically meant that violence in war should be governed by two important norms—proportionality and discrimination (noncombatant immunity). The first norm means that the violence of war should always be limited and proportional to the military objectives; the second means that civilians should not be the primary targets in warfare. Some commentators have suggested that the aim of the just war doctrine has been to justify war, but nothing could be further from the truth. As Holmes has aptly noted, the aim of this approach is not to justify war, but rather to bring it under the control of justice so that, if consistently practiced by disputing states, it would eliminate war altogether.[10]

Most Christians tend to identify implicitly or explicitly with the just war approach. They do so because it seeks to reconcile the problem of international aggression and injustice with the sovereignty of states. In 1983 Gallup conducted for the National Association of Evangelicals an opinion poll of Evangelicals' views on the nuclear arms race. According to the survey, 72 percent of the respondents believed (85 percent if those who had no opinion are excluded) that a person could be a good Christian and support the possession of nuclear arms. Moreover, more than half of the respon-

---

[10]Arthur F. Holmes, "The Just War," in Clouse, *War*, p. 119.

dents indicated that nuclear war was made more likely by the United States falling behind. Only one-fifth of the group thought the arms race itself was a primary cause of nuclear war.[11] Although Evangelicals and other Christians generally agree about the possession of nuclear weapons, there is much less consensus about the strategy for employing such arms. More specifically, there is substantial disagreement as to how to apply the principles of the just war doctrine to strategic nuclear policies.

In recent years there has been an increase in pacifism among North American Protestants and Catholics. As an authentic theological expression of faith, biblical pacifism is an essential element of the church's peacekeeping witness, but it is not the only valid biblical or moral approach. The authority of government, backed by compulsory force, including military violence, is also a legitimate biblical expression. Ideally, Christian pacifists and realists should recognize each other's contributions and work together toward the promotion of a just and peaceful world order. Professor James E. Dougherty has written about the importance of both groups:

> There need be no fundamental contradiction between the call of Christians to work for peace and the obligation of the state to rely upon military power as an instrument to protect the common good for which political leaders are responsible. . . . Neither pacifists nor those who support national defense policies should hold each other in contempt, as they sometimes do. The community which belittles the value of individual witness to the Gospel is likely to fall short in its quest for justice in its foreign and defense policy, and does an injustice to some of its own citizens who are sincere in their consciences. Conversely, the community which ignores the requirements of legitimate defense will not be able to sustain a framework of order where political justice can be made to prevail and where the Gospel message can be lived and preached in freedom.[12]

While my analysis is based largely on a just war perspective, I do not consider it to be the only biblical

---

[11] "Views of Evangelicals on the Nuclear Arms Race," June 1983, Gallup Survey for the National Association of Evangelicals, Washington, D.C.

[12] James E. Dougherty, *The Bishops and Nuclear Weapons* (Hamden, Conn.: Archon Books, 1984), pp. 13–14.

approach. I do believe, however, that the state has a divine role to promote justice and order. The realistic perspective from which this study is written underscores the necessity of public power in pursuit of the common world good. To paraphrase James Madison, there are two challenges in developing a moral national security policy: first, states must have adequate power in order to protect the legitimate interests of citizens and to promote the common good worldwide; second, the power of states must be adequately regulated if it is to serve the cause of peace and justice and not result in imperialism. The challenge, then, in devising a moral nuclear strategy is how to maintain an adequate nuclear policy that promotes the greatest amount of justice with the least evil.

THE MORALITY OF DETERRENCE

There are two important problems involved in developing a moral strategic nuclear policy. The first concerns the legitimacy of threats, and the second, the legitimacy of declaratory policy. The first deals with the morality of threatening the use of nuclear arms; the second concerns the type of threats that should be made, whether explicitly or implicitly.

The Defense of Deterrence

Deterrence is evil. It is evil because it threatens massive destruction. But like war, the doing of evil can be morally justified, provided it is undertaken as the policy occasioning the least amount of evil. The justification for deterrence differs from the justification for war because deterrence concerns threats rather than actual violence.

The case for deterrence rests on four key conditions. First, nuclear technology exists and has been applied to instruments of warfare. The developments of nuclear science cannot be erased, and the eradication of nuclear weapons is wholly unrealistic. The only prudent and morally responsible conduct of U.S. public officials is to accept the reality of nuclear arms. The weapons are here, and the problem is how to manage them in the light of the demands for world peace and international justice.

Second, given their enormous destructive potential, nuclear (atomic), and especially thermonuclear (hydrogen), weapons provide a state with the "ultimate" weapon of national protection. They can provide ultimate protection, for a major threat can be countered by the possible destruction of major portions of the aggressor society. Because Israel is assumed to possess nuclear capabilities, it has enormous military leverage against any Arab states that might wish to eliminate it.

Third, at present there is no defense against nuclear weapons. Moreover, because of the problem of leverage— that is, the relative ease with which nuclear offensive systems can overcome complicated, expensive defenses—it is unlikely that an effective protective system can be developed in the foreseeable future. Deterrence has been accepted because the only available defense against nuclear aggression is the offensive threat of unacceptable retaliation. Since there is no protection against nuclear attack, each of the superpowers is vulnerable to attack; but the vulnerability to retaliation inhibits the possible first use of such weapons.

Fourth, deterrence is accepted because threats and actions, deterrence and nuclear war, bear different moral consequences. Since the degree of "intention" involved in the policy of deterrence can vary significantly, the equating of nuclear war with deterrence is morally and philosophically unwarranted.[13] Deterrence does, of course, bear some of the evil consequences of nuclear war, but Michael Walzer is closer to the truth when he observes that "we threaten evil in order not to do it, and the doing of it would be so terrible that the threat seems in comparison to be morally defensible."[14]

Counterforce Versus Assured Destruction

But what types of threats should be made? Should declaratory policy emphasize limited or unlimited punish-

[13]One of the most complex moral issues surrounding the nuclear dilemma is the question of "intention." A simple but accurate exposition of this problem is set forth by Arthur Hockaday, "In Defense of Deterrence," in Geoffrey Goodwin, ed., *Ethics and Nuclear Deterrence* (New York: St. Martin's, 1982), pp. 83–86. For further discussion of this issue see: Michael Novak, "Moral Clarity in the Nuclear Age," *National Review*, April 1, 1983, pp. 383–86; J. E. Hare and Carey B. Joynt, *Ethics and International Affairs* (New York: St. Martin's, 1982), pp. 101–12; and George Mavrodes, "The Morality of Nuclear Threats," *The Reformed Journal* 32 (Sept. 1982).

[14]Michael Walzer, *Just and Unjust Wars* (New York: Basic Books, 1977), p. 382.

ment, military or civilian targets? This is a difficult and much debated topic. At the risk of oversimplification, there have been two dominant approaches to nuclear strategy in the United States during the past twenty-five years—counterforce and assured destruction. The latter approach, also known as mutual assured destruction (M.A.D.), assumes that nuclear arms are fundamentally indiscriminate and that no amount of refinement in targeting and weapons development can alter their character. Nuclear weapons are so destructive that the preeminent, if not sole, objective of nuclear strategy is to inhibit major aggression by threatening unacceptable retaliation. Bernard Brodie, an influential nuclear strategist, observed shortly after the end of the Second World War that the major military problem in the future was not winning nuclear wars but ensuring that such conflicts would not occur. In *The Absolute Weapon* Brodie wrote:

> The first and most vital step in any American program for the age of atomic bombs is to take measures to guarantee to ourselves in case of attack the possibility of retaliation in kind. The writer in making this statement is not for the moment concerned about who will win the next war in which atomic bombs are used. Thus far the chief purpose of our military establishment has been to win wars. From now on its chief purpose must be to avert them. It can have almost no other useful purpose.[15]

Assured destruction is concerned not with flexibility and accuracy of retaliation, but with the certainty of unacceptable punishment. This approach, therefore, has generally emphasized major retaliatory strikes on key military and civilian targets.

The counterforce approach, by contrast, assumes that the credibility of deterrence is based on the maintenance of a wide variety of retaliatory options, from accurate, limited nuclear strikes to massive retaliation. There are two key features of this approach—flexibility of retaliation and the targeting of military and political centers. Counterforce developed in the early 1960s out of an effort to improve the credibility of threats by making them more limited and accurate and also out of the conviction that maintaining a nuclear strategy based on the indiscriminate destruction of

---

[15] Bernard Brodie, "War in the Atomic Age," in B. Brodie, ed., *The Absolute Weapon* (New York: Harcourt Brace, 1946), p. 76.

civilian population centers was immoral. In 1973 political scientist Fred Iklé criticized the assured destruction policy of the United States by arguing that the indiscriminate threats posed by M.A.D. was morally perverse.

> The jargon of American strategic analysis works like a narcotic. It dulls our sense of moral outrage about the tragic confrontation of nuclear arsenals, primed and constantly perfected to unleash widespread genocide. . . . It blinds us to the fact that our method for preventing nuclear war rests on a form of warfare universally condemned since the Dark Ages—the mass killing of hostages. . . . Indeed, our nuclear strategy is supposed to work the better, the larger the number of hostages that would pay with their lives should the strategy fail.[16]

The goal of counterforce, or what was originally called flexible response, was thus to "purify" nuclear strategy by making it less morally objectionable. Whether or not the evolution of American strategy has become more moral is doubtful.

The counterforce approach appears to be morally preferable at first glance because it has the potential of limiting civilian casualties in the event that deterrence fails. The refinement of nuclear strategy also comes at a significant moral cost—namely, the weakening of deterrence and the making of limited nuclear war more possible. Since the level of the threat is inversely related to the probability of use, the shift toward counterforce decreases the potential level of destruction but increases the potential of nuclear war. The increased possibility of using nuclear weapons derives from the weakening of psychological barriers against using such arms. This shift in psychological inhibitions has been especially encouraged by strategists such as Colin Grey and Keith Payne, who have suggested that an effective nuclear strategy must have a military plan for winning.[17] The nuclear war-fighting strategy—an extreme version of the counterforce approach—assumes that nuclear weapons can be used as instruments of warfare. Such an approach is clearly morally unacceptable. While there may be a moral imperative to limit

---

[16] Fred C. Iklé, "Can Nuclear Deterrence Last Out the Century?" *Foreign Affairs*, Jan. 1973, p. 281.

[17] See Colin Grey and Keith Payne, "Victory Is Possible," *Foreign Affairs* 39 (Summer 1980).

the loss of civilian life during international hostilities, an even greater moral challenge is to assure that nuclear weapons are never used. Whatever the strategy and targeting doctrine of nuclear strategy, it is crucial that we make sure that nuclear conflict does not occur. The chief moral mandate in the nuclear age is to avoid nuclear war.

THE BISHOPS' PASTORAL LETTER

In May of 1983 the U.S. Catholic bishops adopted a pastoral letter on nuclear weapons titled *The Challenge of Peace*. This document, which Father Theodore Hesburgh of Notre Dame has called "the finest document the American Catholic hierarchy has ever produced,"[18] is significant because it is the most thorough study of the problem by any church or religious organization and also because it is one of the most careful applications of just war theory to the problems of the nuclear age. Numerous other religious organizations have developed similar documents on the morality of U.S. nuclear strategy, and several Protestant denominations have issued resolutions condemning the arms race and reliance on nuclear weapons, but these efforts have been largely superficial. The pastoral letter, by contrast, is a carefully crafted document, the result of a long-term drafting process involving much informed discussion and debate. We shall briefly examine and analyze the bishops' letter here, for it illustrates and illuminates some of the major moral issues involved in the ambiguous and paradoxical policy of deterrence.

The Argument

The central argument of the pastoral letter is that nuclear deterrence is conditionally acceptable. The bishops' argument is based on several key principles or realities: First, nuclear weapons are qualitatively different from conventional arms and do not provide usable military force. Second, nuclear war is wholly wrong. The letter states: "Traditionally, the church's moral teaching sought first to prevent war and then to limit its consequences if it occurred. Today the possibilities for placing political and moral limits on nuclear

---

[18]Theodore M. Hesburgh, foreward in Philip Murnion, ed., *Catholics and Nuclear War* (New York: Crossroad, 1983), p. vii.

war are so minimal that the moral task . . . is prevention."[19] Third, given the moral imperative to avoid nuclear war, there can be no justification for the first use of nuclear weapons. Conventional aggression must be repulsed with conventional arms. The only moral justification for using nuclear weapons is prior nuclear aggression. Fourth, maintaining a nuclear deterrent is an imperfect yet effective way of defending the just interests of states in the international system. The bishops state that reliance on a system of balance of power, especially a balance of nuclear power, can serve only as a temporary instrument of peacekeeping. Its justification is conditional because it cannot serve as a permanent basis for peace. The support for deterrence is thus a "minimum" condition based on the recognition that it can only provide a temporary and imperfect peace.

One of the important themes of the pastoral letter is that not all forms of deterrence are moral. If deterrence is to be conditionally legitimate, it must conform to the principles of the just war doctrine, especially the principles of discrimination and proportionality. According to the bishops, the policies of assured destruction and counterforce are both unjustified, for neither can be reconciled fully with the just war principles. Assured destruction is immoral because it implicitly targets civilian populations; counterforce, by contrast, is unacceptable because it increases the possibility of nuclear war and thereby threatens the principle of proportionality. In the end, therefore, the pastoral letter presents a paradox: it affirms deterrence, but it weakens, if not denies, the only strategies available for its implementation.

Shortcomings of the Letter

As I have argued elsewhere,[20] the bishops' failure to provide a morally satisfactory answer to the problem of deterrence derives from their effort to reconcile the just war doctrine with the realities of nuclear strategy. Bruce Russett writes that if deterrence is to be morally legitimate, it must pass the same moral standards as war.[21] But why must this

---

[19] U.S. Catholic Bishops, "The Challenge of Peace: God's Promise and Our Response," the pastoral letter on war and peace, *Origins,* May 19, 1983, 13.II.A.

[20] Mark R. Amstutz, "The Challenge of Peace: Did the Bishops Help?" *This World* 11 (Spring/Summer 1985): 22–35.

[21] Bruce M. Russett, "Ethical Dilemmas of Nuclear Deterrence," *International Security* 8 (Spring 1984): 51.

be the case? Are not threats and actions different? Do not war and deterrence bear different moral consequences? If deterrence is to be properly assessed morally, the inherent limitations of the just war doctrine to nuclear strategy must be recognized. Just war is about war, not about deterrence. Deterrence is about how to avoid war altogether. It is a preface to war. The bishops' failure to recognize this truth contributed to an ambiguous pastoral letter affirming a temporal peace based on conditional deterrence. But the letter's analysis ultimately weakens nuclear deterrence, thereby threatening the quest for peace that the letter is ostensibly promoting. Since nuclear conflict and deterrence are inversely related, the strengthening of deterrence increases the likelihood of peace, while the weakening of deterrence increases the possibility of nuclear conflict. Curiously, the bishops seek to break new ground by promoting a weak deterrent and a stable world order simultaneously. Regrettably, they cannot have it both ways.

The pastoral letter is an impressive though disappointing document. It is impressive because it is the most significant church document on the nuclear dilemma and certainly one of the most careful public policy documents ever issued by a church. The letter provides a valuable analysis of the biblical basis of peacekeeping and an excellent moral assessment of nuclear strategy. At the same time, the letter does not successfully resolve the moral paradox of deterrence, nor does it reconcile the realities of nuclear power with the legitimate claims of national defense. The bishops have argued that nuclear war is unacceptable; they have also affirmed the conditional legitimacy of deterrence. However, by applying the moral standards of just war to deterrence, they have undermined the only policy available for ultimately protecting just interests of the United States and promoting liberty worldwide.

APPROACHES TO PEACE

Disarmament Versus Arms Control

Historically, there have been two basic approaches to nuclear peacekeeping—disarmament and arms control. Disarmament is based on the idea that the most effective way of promoting peace is to reduce and hopefully eliminate the instruments of warfare. This approach is opposed to deterrence because it assumes that the continued reliance on such a doctrine increases the likelihood of war. Since deterrence requires the continued modernization of nuclear stockpiles and delivery systems, reliance on deterrence fosters an arms race which itself is a source of instability of military political competition. The disarmament approach therefore seeks to promote peace by halting modernization and proliferation of nuclear weapons. An example of a proposal rooted in the quantitative approach of disarmament is the nuclear freeze initiative.

Whereas disarmament rejects the logic of deterrence, arms control accepts the reality of nuclear weapons as an inescapable condition of contemporary world politics. Disarmament seeks to reduce or eliminate the weapons of mass destruction, but arms control assumes that the nuclear arms must be managed in world politics. Because the elimination of nuclear weapons is considered an impossible and unrealistic goal at this time, arms control seeks to reduce the likelihood of nuclear aggression by focusing on the management of weapons systems. The goal of arms control is to regulate the development and deployment of weapons in order to inhibit nuclear war.

A central postulate of arms control is that peace between the United States and the Soviet Union derives from *stable deterrence*—a condition where superpowers assume that first use of strategic nuclear weapons would result in net losses. In order for deterrence to be stable, three conditions need to exist: first, population and industrial centers need to be vulnerable to attack; second, nuclear forces must be relatively invulnerable; and third, strategic forces must be able to carry out unacceptable punishment against aggressor states. What is important in achieving stability is not the scope of destruction, but rather the certainty of carrying out retaliation after suffering a nuclear attack.

As a Christian, it is easier to identify with disarmament than with arms control.[22] But however tempting disarmament may be, only arms control provides a morally prudent

---

[22] Some of the appeals of disarmament include: (1) it rejects deterrence as a tolerable solution, even in the short-run; (2) it rejects all reliance on nuclear weapons; and (3) it provides a simple, unambiguous peace formula.

approach to the nuclear dilemma. It is the only approach that addresses the problem of peacekeeping in the light of the enormous destructive power of fifty thousand nuclear warheads. Even if both superpowers were to drastically reduce the size of their nuclear arsenals, the existence of several thousand weapons would still pose a much more serious threat to civilization than all conventional military power combined. Thus, while the reduction of the number of nuclear warheads is an important goal, an even more fundamental challenge is to ensure that no nuclear warhead is ever released. The energies of Christian peacemakers need to be focused on how to maintain strategic stability in the midst of continued political and technological threats to this condition.

The stability of superpower nuclear arsenals can be threatened in a variety of ways. These include political crises between the United States and the Soviet Union and scientific innovations in weaponry resulting in either a more vulnerable strategic deterrent or in decreased capabilities for retaliating against nuclear aggressors. Developments that might impede stability include civil defense programs, production of highly accurate but less-destructive nuclear weapons, and deployment of antiballistic missile systems. Such developments may be counterproductive, for they could contribute to the illusion that nuclear weapons can be used as instruments of warfare and that meaningful defense is possible in the nuclear age. Similarly, the deployment of first-strike weapons—that is, weapons that can threaten the land-based strategic weapons of others states (basically ICBMs and some bombers)—is also harmful to strategic stability, for they threaten the strategic weapons designed for retaliation. Although difficult to comprehend, the development of defensive systems along with more accurate missile warheads can be harmful to the quest for peace. To the extent that the imperfect peace between the superpowers derives from the stability of strategic deterrence, developments which threaten any of the requirements of this condition must be deemed harmful. This is why invulnerability of strategic weapons is important but why defense of civilian population centers is not. "Weapons aimed at people lessen the risk of war," notes Charles Krauthammer; "weapons aimed at weapons, increase it."[23]

The superpowers need to reduce both the number and destructive potential of their nuclear arsenals. It is especially important to reduce the number of nuclear warheads. The major threat to nuclear stability lies in the growing imbalance between the number of Soviet warheads and the number of U.S. land-based strategic missiles. This threat has been made possible by the development of accurate guidance systems combined with the deployment of hydraheaded missiles known as MIRVs (multiple-independent re-entry vehicles). As the ratio of warheads to land-based missiles has increased, strategic stability has declined.[24] Arms control experts therefore have advocated the reduction of MIRVed missiles threatening ICBMs. A major aim of the Reagan administration Strategic Arms Reduction Talks (START) was to do exactly that.

Nuclear Offense Versus Nuclear Defense

Since 1983 there has been much discussion in the United States about the possible development of a strategic defense system to replace the offensive strategy of M.A.D. This discussion has been prompted by the Reagan administration's strategic defense initiative (S.D.I.), or what the media has called "star wars." As articulated by administration officials, the aim of the S.D.I. is to explore the technical feasibility of developing a defensive system which would render nuclear weapons obsolete. The S.D.I. is morally attractive, for it seeks to shift the emphasis of nuclear strategy from offense to defense. S.D.I. proponents share with disarmament idealists the vision of a denuclearized world—an environment where nuclear weapons no longer play a decisive role in world politics, where deterrence has ceased to be important. There has been much speculation

---

[23]Charles Krauthammer, "The Real Way to Prevent Nuclear War," *The New Republic*, April 28, 1982, p. 15.

[24]Because of the increasing threat posed to U.S. land-based missiles, President Reagan constituted a commission in 1983 to examine the problem of the vulnerability of U.S. ICBMs. The report of the commission, headed by Brent Scowcroft, said that it was impossible to adequately defend land-based missiles from Soviet attack. The problem of missile vulnerability, according to the Scowcroft Commission report, is therefore not subject to technical resolution—not at least in the foreseeable future.

about the possibility of developing a sufficiently reliable and comprehensive system, but even if such a system could be developed at great expense, is such a shift morally desirable? Three important reasons have been given for pursuing the S.D.I.: (1) to provide a partial defensive system for our land-based missiles in order to shore up deterrence, (2) to provide a comprehensive defense for military and population centers against strategic nuclear attack, and (3) to provide a "bargaining chip" in the arms control process. A limited-point defense system, in accordance with the 1972 Antiballistic Missile treaty, could certainly provide some protection to the increasingly vulnerable land-based missile force. But the exploration of strategic defense—estimated at more than $30 billion during its early phases—would seem to be an enormously wasteful use of resources simply to enhance arms control bargaining. The chief problem of the S.D.I., however, is not that it fails to strengthen deterrence or that it is too expensive; its major limitation is that it seeks to transcend deterrence through a defensive system rendering strategic nuclear weapons obsolete. Defense would replace nuclear offense.

Fundamentally, the S.D.I. weakens deterrence by holding to a romantic ideal of world peace, in which nuclear weapons lose their usefulness. The effort to overcome the moral limitations of M.A.D. are laudable, but as I suggested earlier, idealism has its limitations and dangers. The S.D.I. seeks to overcome the pain, danger, and ugliness of nuclear strategy by developing a system that would render nuclear offense useless. It seeks, in other words, a radical transformation in the strategy of peacekeeping.

The danger of such radical idealism is that it shifts attention away from the present realities to a less dangerous and hostile world. But as Leon Wieseltier has observed, "Nobody likes the danger we are in. But more dangerous still is the distraction from the danger."[25]

The vision of a world where nuclear offense has been replaced by defense involves as great a leap of faith as radical disarmament proposals. Nuclear pacifists and the proponents of space defense initiatives share a common abhorrence of M.A.D. Both the adherents of strategic defense and

<hr>

[25] Leon Wieseltier, "Nuclear Idealism, Nuclear Realism," *The New Republic,* March 11, 1985, p. 25.

nuclear disarmament assume that assured destruction is an immoral strategy which must be reformed. But whereas disarmament seeks to eliminate weapons systems altogether, the strategic defense proposal seeks to replace nuclear offense with an antinuclear defensive system.

PEACEKEEPING PROPOSALS

I have argued that Christians are called to be agents of peace. I also suggested earlier that Christians are called to promote international justice. Both the quest for peace and justice will require the authority and power of government. The invention of nuclear technology has radically transformed world politics because it has provided a few states with instruments of mass, indiscriminate destruction. Since nuclear weapons are not in themselves immoral, the pacifist alternative of unilateral renunciation is unrealistic and irresponsible. The basic tasks of Christian peacemakers are to influence the development and implementation of U.S. security policies so that they provide adequate national defense, and, at the same time, to promote world justice. These tasks must be carried out in ways that reduce the possibility of nuclear war.

I have pointed out that the fundamental aim of nuclear weapons is deterrence. Since not all expressions of deterrence are morally legitimate, Christians must support policies that increase the stability of deterrence and also reduce the threat of nuclear war. There is no immediate alternative to the balance of terror, so our challenge is to promote simultaneously arms control and political and military conditions that foster world order. World peace will not be automatically advanced by those who cry for peace, rather it will result from the development of wise and moral policies. Former President Nixon has written about the dangers of confusing an idealistic and realistic peace:

> Confusing real peace with perfect peace is a dangerous but common fallacy. Because of the realities of human nature, perfect peace is achieved in two places only: in the grave and at the typewriter. Perfect peace is the stuff of poetry and high-minded newspaper editorials. Real peace, on the other hand, will be the down-to-earth product of the real world, manufactured by realistic,

calculating leaders whose sense of their nations' self-interest is diamond-hard and unflinching.[26]

I will conclude with a number of specific recommendations that can contribute to a more moral and effective U.S. nuclear policy.

1. *Declaration of "no first use."* The United States should adopt a no-first-use nuclear policy. Ideally, the United States should declare a no-first-use policy for both conventional and nuclear weapons, but as an interim policy it would be wise to affirm the more limited doctrine. Such a policy would be consistent with the aim of Western democracies, which is to use power defensively to protect moral interests. In addition, such an announcement would be to affirm a clear and limited purpose for nuclear weapons—namely, to deter nuclear aggression. Currently, U.S. policy seeks to deter more than nuclear attack. The problem with a broader conception of deterrence is that it potentially weakens deterrence and increases the possibility of nuclear war. This is why the Catholic bishops' pastoral letter strongly endorses the limited role of deterrence. They recommend that nonnuclear attacks by other states should be resisted by other than nuclear means.

A growing number of arms control experts have suggested that the United States should publicly renounce first use. Four former distinguished public officials have written a highly influential article in which they advocate the adoption of this policy. According to them, the military conditions have changed radically in Western Europe in the past twenty-five years since the integration of nuclear and conventional defensive strategies were first developed. To the extent that conventional arms imbalances contribute to a weak deterrence, the authors suggest that these should be solved not by depending on nuclear weapons, but by strengthening conventional defenses. "What the Alliance needs most," they write, "is not the refinement of its nuclear options, but a clear cut decision to avoid them as long as others do."[27]

---

[26]Richard Nixon, "Is Peace Possible?" *The New York Times,* Oct. 2, 1983, sec. 4, p. 19.

[27]McGeorge Bundy, George F. Kennan, Robert McNamara, and Gerard Smith, "Nuclear Weapons and the Atlantic Alliance," *Foreign Affairs,* April 1982, pp. 753–68. For a response to this article, see Karl Kaiser, Georg

2. *Comprehensive test ban.* The purpose of the Limited Test Ban of 1963 was to seek control over the level of nuclear explosions. This was done by limiting such explosions to underground tests. Subsequently, the United States and Soviet Union agreed to limit such tests to less than 150 kilotons of power. As an instrument of regulating the number of explosions, the 1963 treaty has not been successful. Prior to 1963 there was an average of twenty-seven tests per year; since the ratification of the treaty, the number of nuclear tests has risen to forty-five per year. To date more than twelve hundred explosions have taken place, with nearly 90 percent of these being carried out by the United States, the Soviet Union, and Great Britain.

The purpose of a comprehensive test ban is to bring a halt to all nuclear explosions. Since the superpowers have too many nuclear warheads already, further testing can contribute little to effective deterrence. It will not strengthen the stability of deterrence. Indeed, continued testing will only exacerbate tensions between nuclear and nonnuclear states and further suspicions between the superpowers. Moreover, the development of smaller, more efficient nuclear warheads will only further weaken the "firebreak"[28] between nuclear and conventional weapons.

3. *Reduction of tactical nuclear arms.* Tactical nuclear weapons differ from the strategic systems (ICBMs, SLBMs, and bombers) in that they are smaller, less destructive, and designed for battlefield use. Originally developed for the defense of Western Europe, tactical weapons have become an integral part of U.S. military forces throughout the world. While reliance on tactical nuclear weapons provided NATO in the 1950s and 1960s with a comparatively inexpensive way of countering substantially superior conventional Warsaw Pact forces, dependence on such weapons has had one significant cost—it has increased the risk of nuclear conflict. It has done so by integrating tactical nuclear weapons into

---

Leber, Alois Mertes, and Franz-Josef Schulze, "Nuclear Weapons and the Preservation of Peace: A German Response" and "The Debate Over No First Use" (letters), *Foreign Affairs*, Summer 1982, pp. 1157–80.

[28] A "firebreak" is that area of land surrounding a forest fire which is cleared and plowed in order to contain the fire. The concept is applied in nuclear strategy to denote that psychological line of demarcation between "usable" and "nonusable" military forces, nuclear and conventional weapons.

the war-fighting strategies of NATO, with the result that the nuclear threshold or firebreak between nuclear and conventional weapons has been lowered. The weakening of the psychological line of demarcation between conventional and nuclear forces, usable and deterrent forces, has led inevitably to a weakening of deterrence. The United States should make every effort to maintain nuclear weapons as forces of ultimate resort. It is in the national interest to reduce the number of tactical weapons, especially from the forward-base areas in West Germany, and to reform defensive strategies to avoid dependence on such weapons at all. The decision to use nuclear weapons should never be made at the battlefield level. The threat posed by intermediate and long-range strategic weapons is more than sufficient to maintain a credible deterrent.

4. *Strengthening of the command and control of nuclear weapons.* Although the U.S. Department of Defense has sought in recent years to improve the security and communications systems related to nuclear weapons, much more needs to be done. In the light of the enormous destructive potential of strategic weapons, it is essential to ensure their safety against accidental or unauthorized use and to maintain effective, reliable surveillance systems. At the same time, if deterrence is to be credible and stable, a reliable communications system must exist to direct and control U.S. strategic forces after a surprise nuclear attack.

5. *Reduction of strategic nuclear warheads.* Currently, both the Soviet Union and the United States have nearly ten thousand strategic warheads each. Since several hundred of such weapons have more destructive power than all weapons used in the First and Second World Wars, it is difficult to comprehend how the continued addition of warheads increases national security generally and the credibility of deterrence in particular. To be sure, the dispersion of nuclear power with the triad (land-based and sea-based missiles and bombers) has enhanced deterrence. But strategic stability can be achieved at substantially lower levels of warheads. The Reagan administration proposal to lower the number of warheads to five thousand for each superpower can contribute to the stability of world order.

But the requirements of a stable world need to be reinforced by another important reform: the replacement of MIRVed missiles with single-warhead missiles. Expansion of warheads has been made possible by the development of hydraheaded missiles that permit a single missile to carry from three to fourteen separate warheads. This development has been harmful because it has created a potential threat to the security of strategic forces. The threat arises from the fact that a small portion of the strategic forces can threaten, with a first strike, the land-based strategic weapons of another state. It is therefore important not only to reduce the number of missiles and warheads but also the ratio of warheads to launchers. Only then will the potential threat of first strike be eased.

6. *Strengthening of nonproliferation programs.* One of the most dangerous threats to world peace lies in the proliferation of nuclear weapons to other nations or groups. The potential for acquisition of nuclear devices by terrorists is one of the most frightening developments to arise from the application of nuclear technology to military weaponry. Roger Molander, a former U.S. National Security advisor, has said: "I used to think that U.S.–Soviet arms control was the Mt. Everest of earthly problems. But that was before I understood nuclear proliferation. It makes the superpower arms race look like a comparatively minor league problem."[29]

If the world is to remain safe, nuclear states need to inhibit the spreading of nuclear weapons-making capabilities. The United States and its allies need to apply great discipline in the export of nuclear technology—certainly more than they have in the past. To strengthen nuclear nonproliferation, the United States should: (1) encourage strict adherence to the nonproliferation treaty, which calls on nonmember states to forswear nuclear-weapons developments in exchange for assistance with power programs; (2) encourage states that have not ratified the treaty, especially those with nuclear capabilities, to do so; and (3) monitor the nuclear capabilities of revolutionary regimes and terrorist groups to ensure that they do not acquire nuclear bombs.

Arms control initiatives such as these will not themselves guarantee peace or prevent an outbreak of nuclear conflict, but coupled with the development of harmonious political relationships, such policies can increase the poten-

---

[29] "Who Has the Bomb?" *Time*, June 3, 1985, p. 11.

tial for peace between the superpowers. In the final analysis, peace is God's gift to the world. Christians must work fervently for the establishment of sound public policies and pray for the transformation of men and women and of the states they inhabit.

5

PROMOTING HUMAN RIGHTS

"It is better to keep the sources of moral judgment alive in the national life at the cost of hypocrisy than it is to lower the proclaimed standards to the practice of the moment."

John C. Bennett[1]

"Men have not lived as brothers. They have not treated each other as equals. They have recognized no common human family or destiny. They have repeatedly outraged the rights and dignity of fellowmen. War, conquest, enslavement, massacre, and pillage make up all too much of the wretched chronicle of human affairs. How, then, do we argue that these savage, murderous animals, hunting each other in cruel packs, are brothers, equal, responsible, and of incomprehensible value and human worth?"

Barbara Ward[2]

The world, as Nicholas Wolterstorff has pointed out, is a place of many "sorrows."[3] Some of these sorrows have their root in the unjust and fallen nature of the world political system, but many of them are rooted in the corrupt and

[1]John C. Bennett, *Foreign Policy in Christian Perspective* (New York: Scribner, 1966), p. 13.

[2]Barbara Ward, *The Lopsided World* (New York: Norton, 1968), p. 22.

[3]Nicholas Wolterstorff, *Until Justice and Peace Embrace* (Grand Rapids: Eerdmans, 1983), p. 42.

exploitative practices and policies of nations. We observed in chapter 3 that a basic moral principle of the existing international order is the sovereignty of states and the corollary duty of nonintervention. Obviously, if all states pursued justice and affirmed human dignity, there would be no need to explore the moral responsibilities of states toward other regimes.

But governments do commit evil. Many wantonly abuse, torture, and kill people, imprison citizens without cause, and persecute minorities and religious groups. The following are some contemporary examples of governmental barbarity.

In 1972, Burundi, a small, landlocked African nation, embarked on a massive extermination campaign to eliminate the Hutu people. Nearly a quarter of a million Hutus perished under the brutal regime of the Tutsi rulers.

In nearby Uganda, Idi Amin's military regime is said to have killed more than two hundred thousand Ugandans in his consolidation of political power in the mid 1970s. The unremitting evil was stopped only when Tanzania declared war on Uganda and helped bring down Amin's government.

From 1975 until 1979 the communist Khmer Rouge, led by Pol Pot, carried out the most destructive genocide campaign since Hitler's extermination campaign against Jews. While there is wide disagreement about the exact number of people who perished in Kampuchea during this four-year period, it is generally estimated that a minimum of two million persons were either killed directly by the Khmer Rouge or died from starvation.

While the military was in power in Argentina in the 1970s, a minimum of seven thousand people "disappeared" and perished at the hands of military and police forces.

In 1982, in an effort to consolidate power, the ruling Sandinistas in Nicaragua embarked on a forcible relocation of its Misquito Indians. Thousands refused to obey and fled to refugee camps in neighboring Honduras.

The totalitarian regimes in China, Cuba, and the Soviet Union continue to hold tens of thousands of political prisoners—prisoners whose only crime was to express ideas and convictions contrary to the ruling communist party.

Although some reforms have been instituted in recent years in South Africa, the country's political system is still based on the practice of apartheid. Fundamentally, the country's political system is based on the doctrine of racial inequality, with political and economic power being controlled by whites.

What should the Department of State's policy be on evils such as these? Should the United States publicly denounce states that commit human rights violations? Should it deny them military and economic assistance? Should an economic embargo be carried out against them? If policies such as these do not work, should the United States protect people through humanitarian intervention? Is democracy essential for human dignity? Should our government promote democracy abroad? If so, how? While the scope of this study does not permit an answer to each of these questions, I want to explore the general problem of promoting human rights in foreign lands, focusing on the limits and possibilities of a moral human rights policy. Because Christians hold to a transcendent view of people, they have a special obligation to uphold and affirm human rights.

The aim of this chapter is to examine how the U.S. government can improve human dignity worldwide through its bilateral and multilateral policies. First, I shall define human rights and explore the relationship of faith to basic rights. I shall then examine the relationship of human rights to democracy; and finally, I shall set forth principles and guidelines for developing a modest, prudential human rights strategy for the promotion of basic rights.

THE NATURE OF HUMAN RIGHTS

Most people think they know what human rights are. They are the purposes for which governments exist. Yet the familiarity with the concept of rights may be an impediment to understanding what basic human rights entail. Augustine once declared, "If one asks me what it is, I know; if called upon to explain, I do not know." This is especially applicable to our knowledge of human rights. We know what human rights are, but it is difficult to explain what they are to others. It is important, therefore, to define the concept of rights with care and to apply it to the conduct of foreign policy with unusual caution.

The Moral Basis of Rights

One of the dangers of defining and promoting basic rights is the tendency to define rights in terms of a particular culture and a contemporary historical epoch. Although the problems of ethnocentrism and chronological provincialism (believing that what is valid now has always been so) pose major obstacles to the development and implementation of a moral and credible human rights policy, such problems are not insuperable. Indeed, the long-term effectiveness and credibility of U.S. foreign policy will depend in great measure on the ability to define clearly and soberly those fundamental norms that affirm human dignity universally. If this is to be done, it is essential to recognize that the contemporary conceptions of human rights are a result of a long evolutionary process.[4] Although the notion of human dignity is as old as civilization itself, the concept of individual rights is relatively new, dating perhaps from the seventeenth century.

The development and definition of individual human rights began to take concrete shape during the seventeenth and eighteenth centuries with the social contract ideas of Thomas Hobbes, John Locke, and Jean Jacques Rousseau. The central idea of the social contract theory was that human beings had fundamental rights which were defined by certain basic moral laws known as the laws of nature. The Catholic writer Jacques Maritain has written eloquently of the relationship of rights to natural law:

> The human person possesses rights because of the very fact that it is a person, a whole, master of itself and of its acts, and which consequently is not merely a means to an end, but an end, an end which must be treated as such. The dignity of the human person? The expression means nothing if it does not signify that by virtue of natural law, the human person has the right to be respected, is the subject of rights, possesses rights. These are things which are owed to man because of the very fact that he is man.[5]

The application of natural law to individual rights was a radical and revolutionary idea, especially since morality had been used throughout most of Western civilization to define the common community good, not the individual welfare of

---

[4]For an excellent historical overview of the idea of human rights see Eugene Kamenka's "The Anatomy of an Idea," in Eugene Kamenka and Alice Ehr-Soon Tay, eds., *Human Rights* (London: Edward Arnold, 1978), pp. 1–35.

[5]Jacques Maritain, *The Rights of Man* (London: Centenary, 1944), p. 37.

citizens. The shift in focus from community responsibilities to individual rights was facilitated in great measure by the Renaissance, which contributed to the evolution of a more secular and individualistic society. While the development and evolution of the doctrine of human rights has been based largely on Western thought, we ought not to define or associate human rights exclusively with the modern Western conception of individual rights. Human dignity, after all, has been defined and achieved in a wide variety of human cultures and circumstances. As I will argue later on, while the civil and political rights associated with democracy are of fundamental import, the basic rights of personal security and integrity are even more basic.

The Scriptures are not explicit about the subject of human rights. To a significant degree, the Bible identifies human dignity not with the fulfillment of individual rights and wants, but with human duties and responsibilities to God and to others. At the same time, the Bible affirms human dignity in general and human rights in particular, by giving persons a special and central role in Creation. The Bible teaches that God created people in his own image and that they therefore have a unique distinctive role in the created order. The papal encyclical *Peace on Earth* says that because man is created in the image of God, he has "endowed him with intelligence and freedom." "By virtue of this fact," the encyclical continues, "man has rights and duties of his own, flowing directly and simultaneously from his very nature, which are therefore universal, inviolable and inalienable."[6]

Because of its implicit affirmation of human dignity, the Christian faith has been one of the major forces propelling the doctrine of human rights throughout modern history. The Christian faith has made two specific contributions. First, by emphasizing the worth and dignity of every person, it has implicitly affirmed the doctrine of human equality. Second, by emphasizing the existence of universal, transcendent norms, it has affirmed the limited character of government. The existence of transcendent standards has meant that individuals are subject to two authorities—God and the state, the Creator and government—and that no temporal ruler can legitimately claim complete allegiance

---

[6]Pope John XXIII, *Peace on Earth*, April 11, 1963, art. 9.

from citizens. Because human beings are ultimately subject to God, allegiance to government is always conditional ("We must obey God rather than men!" [Acts 5:29]). The scriptural teaching of the conditional character of temporal authority has proved to be one of the most important and revolutionary developments of modern political thought. It clearly proved to be a major impetus in the development of the doctrine of human rights.

Definition

With these preliminary perspectives in mind, let us define human rights as those rights which derive from the inherent dignity of people.[7] Basic rights are not duties or obligations, but entitlements. To have rights is to possess particular claims that can be asserted, pressed, demanded, and exercised. They are, in the words of Henry Shue, "social shields"[8] for the defense of all individuals. Such rights do not derive from the laws promulgated by governments, but from their inherent moral validity, grounded in the fact of God's creation and sovereignty. Indeed, the duties and responsibilities of government are themselves derivative of these moral claims of individuals. Human rights, in the words of Richard Neuhaus, are "prior rights."[9] The notion of inherent rights is succinctly captured by the Declaration of Independence, which affirms that human dignity is dependent on the protection of life within the context of a community based on equality and liberty. The Declaration states the basic moral principles of human rights as follows: "We hold these truths to be self-evident, that all men are created equal and that they are endowed by their Creator with certain inalienable rights, that among these are life, liberty and the pursuit of happiness."

There is a great deal of confusion in modern society

---

[7] There is an enormous amount of literature on the nature of human rights. Some of the most useful studies include Maurice Cranston, *What Are Human Rights?* (New York: Basic Books, 1962); Jorge Dominguez, Nigel Rodley, Bryce Wood, and Richard Falk, *Enhancing Global Human Rights* (New York: McGraw-Hill, 1979); Louis Henkin, *The Rights of Man Today* (Boulder: Westview, 1978); and Henry Shue, *Basic Rights* (Princeton: Princeton University Press, 1980).

[8] Henry Shue, "In the American Tradition, Rights Remain Unalienable," *The Center Magazine*, Jan.–Feb. 1984, p. 8.

[9] Richard J. Neuhaus, "Christianity and Democracy" (Institute on Religion and Democracy, 1981), p. 8.

about human rights. Much of it is the result of the dilution of the concept of rights in recent decades. One of the reasons for this is the increasing acceptance of social and economic entitlements as part of human rights. This development has been brought about in large measure by the growing influence of the Marxist-socialist ideals of communal life based on socioeconomic rights and by the increasing public expectation that government should provide material care for people. The increasing ability of modern states to provide welfare to the poor has altered people's attitudes and expectations toward government and conception of basic rights. The result has been confusion over the meaning of human rights and an uncertainty as to which rights are basic and which ones are not.[10]

The intellectual confusion surrounding human rights is well illustrated by the Universal Declaration of Human Rights, a document adopted by the United Nations General Assembly in 1948.[11] While this declaration has no legal binding force on states, it has served as the unofficial world charter of human rights. Regrettably, the declaration confuses rather than clarifies the complex subject of human rights. It does so because it defines rights in lofty, all-embracing terms, covering cultural, social, political, and

_____

[10] Do people have a right to medical care, to a job, to a vacation? Do people have a right to emigrate to other countries, and do states have a duty to accept immigrants? Do people have the right to vote, to political participation? Are these rights morally equivalent? In addition to the debate over rights themselves, there is a dispute on the grounding of rights. Robert Goldwin (see R. Goldwin, "Human Rights: The Moral Foundation for American Foreign Policy?" *Discourses* 3 [1978], Loyola University of Chicago) argues that the foundation of human rights lies in the character of regime established in a nation; Charles Beitz ("Human Rights and Social Justice," in Peter G. Brown and Douglas MacLean, eds., *Human Rights and U.S. Foreign Policy* [Lexington: Lexington Books, 1979]) argues that rights are rooted in social justice; and Jack Donnelly ("Human Rights as Natural Rights," *Human Rights Quarterly* 4 [August 1982]) argues that rights are based on natural law.

[11] The declaration includes three basic categories of rights. The first, called fundamental, includes such rights as life, liberty, and security of people (art. 3), freedom from torture (art. 5), freedom from arbitrary arrest and detention (art. 9), and freedom to emigrate (art. 13). The second group, civil-political rights, includes freedom of opinion and expression (art. 19), freedom of peaceful assembly (art. 20), the right of political participation (art. 21), and equal protection under the law (art. 7). The last category includes socioeconomic rights, such as the right to social security (art. 22), the right to work and receive "equal pay for equal work" (art. 23), the right to an adequate standard of living (art. 25), and the right to an education (art. 26).

economic areas. This all-embracing approach to human rights has been accepted not only by international organizations and by many Western developed states, but also by the U.S. government and specifically the U.S. Department of State. In 1977, shortly after President Jimmy Carter assumed office, Secretary of State Cyrus Vance sought to explain the U.S. human rights foreign policy. In a famous speech given at the University of Georgia Law School, Vance defined human rights as the right to be free from governmental abuse; the right of fulfilling vital needs, including food, shelter, health care, and education; and the right to enjoy civil and political liberties.[12]

The problem with this all-inclusive approach to human rights is that it cheapens the notion of human rights and leads to public policy confusion. Since no state can ever fully protect all human rights, an all-embracing definition of rights allows states to focus selectively on some rights and to avoid others. Selective protection of human rights would not be such a grave problem if all rights were equally important. But this is not the case. Some rights are basic; some are not. Thus, when left-wing ideologues compare the human rights records of democratic and totalitarian nations and claim that the Soviet Union has a better record in certain areas of human rights than the United States, they are in principle assuming that there is no moral difference between the two regimes. To be sure, both the United States and the Soviet Union have failed to fully protect human rights. But there is a fundamental distinction between democratic and totalitarian systems, between the limited government of the United States and the expansive, controlling power of the Soviet totalitarian regime.

Rights Versus Goals

If the human rights doctrine is to serve as normative standard for U.S. foreign policy, it is essential to be clear about what basic rights are. To begin with, it is possible to identify three types of rights: fundamental, civil-political, and socioeconomic.

Fundamental or basic rights are rights of personal security. Essentially negative in character, they involve

---

[12] Cyrus Vance, *Human Rights Policy*, Secretary of State, Department of State, Bureau of Public Affairs, April 30, 1977.

protection from the government. Since tyranny has been one of the major violators of basic rights in the history of humankind, the protection from governmental abuse is a fundamental norm of a civilized, moral society. Examples of fundamental rights include protection from abuses such as genocide, systematic use of terror against ethnic or social groups, enslavement, forced labor, persecution of minorities, separation of children from families, and religious persecution.

The second type of right includes civil and political rights associated with the practice of free, constitutional government. These rights, which are rooted in the theory and practice of limited government, are based on law and involve such rights as protection of property, trial by jury, free speech, and other similar liberties found in the Bill of Rights. They also include the right to participate directly or indirectly in government. Political rights include participation in elections through voting, running for office, and campaigning, as well as the right to organize political opposition during and after elections. Political-civil rights are associated primarily with the rise of modern democratic states and, therefore, are not recognized as universal basic rights.

The third type of rights are social and economic entitlements affirmed by modern states. Enshrined by the welfare state, such "positive" rights are best identified as goals, for they are desirable but not necessarily implementable. The "right" to a vacation, a job, or medical care, for example, can enhance human dignity but cannot be interpreted as a universally binding claim, for the ability of societies to fulfill them will depend on a nation's wealth and productive capacities. There can be little doubt that it is morally desirable for governments to promote the common welfare and that, to the extent possible, they should assist and protect weak, suffering people. It is, however, unwise to equate positive and negative rights, especially when the fulfillment of such rights is dependent on the varying capabilities of governments.

To define rights in terms of the contingent ability of regimes is to make basic rights conditional. Either rights are basic, or they are not. They cannot be inalienable and universal if their fulfillment is dependent on national capabilities and resources. This is why the Reagan administration's effort to define socioeconomic rights as goals is essential and prudent. Elliott Abrams, former assistant secretary of state for Human Rights and Humanitarian Affairs, explained the difference between rights and goals as follows:

> In our view, where one person has a right, others have an obligation to respect it. If I have a right to free speech, other individuals and the government must respect and protect that right. Where does this lead with regard to economic and social goals such as good medical care or good housing, or another "right" protected by the Covenant on Economic, Social, and Cultural Rights—paid vacations. To say that the people of Chad or Bangladesh have a right to free speech or press is easily comprehensible. But what can it possibly mean to say they have a "right" to paid vacations? The country and the government are not preventing it, and cannot possibly provide it; the countries are too poor. Does this imply a "right" to foreign aid to finance paid vacations—or medical care or [a home]? No—it implies the view that what we really mean is not that these are "rights" but, rather, highly desirable goals.[13]

The Priority of Basic Rights

Are any of these three categories of rights more fundamental or universal? While I believe that all three types of rights are important to human dignity, only the first type—the rights of personal security—are truly universal. Peter Berger has suggested that, while different religions and cultures have expressed human dignity in a variety of ways, there exists a crosscultural consensus concerning the universality of rights of personal integrity.[14] They are certainly more inclusive than the Western democratic ideals of limited, democratic government and more universally claimed than socioeconomic "rights." The civil and political rights associated with liberal democracies have been indispensable in that they have provided political shields against the exploitation and oppression by governments and individuals. Similarly, the economic expansion of modern societies has done much

[13] Elliott Abrams, "Human Rights and American Foreign Policy, Part IV—Arguments and Afterwords," *The Center Magazine*, July–Aug. 1984, p. 57.

[14] Peter Berger, "Are Human Rights Universal?" *Commentary*, Sept. 1977, pp. 60–63.

to eradicate disease, prolong life, improve living standards, and increase educational opportunities. This has been accomplished partly by the expansion of the welfare state rooted in the doctrine of socioeconomic rights, and, more importantly, in the expansion of the productive capacities of the nation itself. Thus, while democratic and sustenance rights are important to human dignity, the most essential rights are those that relate directly to the integrity and security of persons.

But isolating basic rights from the entitlement goals and civil-political rights is difficult. Basic rights do not arise in a vacuum. They are found within a social, cultural, economic, and political context in which human dignity is protected and enhanced. Just as a prosperous economy is essential to the alleviation of hunger, malnutrition, and poverty, a well-constituted political society is indispensable to basic rights. While I do not claim that a liberal democratic system of government is the only type of regime that can protect human dignity, the institutions of liberal democracy have proven to be history's most benevolent governments and political shields of basic rights. Since governmental tyranny has been the major impediment to human rights historically, the establishment of limited government is essential to human rights. This is why the protection of human rights is directly correlated with democracy. Democracy may not be a sufficient condition for the protection of basic rights, but modern political history suggests that it is a desirable, if not necessary, condition.

The primary threat to basic rights lies in the expansion of totalitarian communism—a political system that seeks to abolish pluralism and threaten human dignity by extinguishing liberty. And if the primary impediment to human rights is communism, its chief alternative is a limited, pluralistic, democratic government. The superpower conflict over political world views is thus not an ancillary tension or dispute, but the most fundamental conflict of our time. How this conflict is managed will determine in great measure the fate of human rights in the future.

DEMOCRACY VERSUS TOTALITARIANISM

The Democratic Alternative

Because of its popular appeal in our contemporary world, many oppressive regimes, including some totalitarian systems (e.g., the Democratic Republic of Germany), have claimed democratic status. To avoid confusion, it is important to define the features of an authentic democracy. Two conditions have generally been identified as essential for democracy: first, there must be widespread participation in the political life; and second, there must be political contestation in the election of government officials. While popular participation is important and relatively easy to achieve in modern societies, the indispensable feature of a democratic nation is the toleration of opposing political forces during and after elections. The litmus test of democracy is whether a "loyal opposition" is tolerated in government and society.

Democracy is not a perfect government. Its decision making is slow and inefficient, the policies of government often lack continuity, and the protection of liberties often results in the toleration of social evils (e.g., pornography) and a relatively low respect for governmental laws and social order. But as Sir Winston Churchill once observed, while democracy is not a very good system of government, it is much better than any other available alternative.

Democracy is the most effective political regime devised to date for protecting basic human rights. It is the most effective system not because of its lofty principles and claims to inalienable, moral rights, but because it has permitted the institutionalization of limited, constitutional government. The irony of democracy is that it protects rights not by doing certain deeds or providing certain goods, but by affirming human rights through the protection of a differentiated, pluralistic society. As Robert Goldwin points out, the protection of rights does not depend on the good will or generosity or even morality of public officials. Rather it depends primarily "on division and distributions of powers; diversity within the society; and enterprising competing spirit of the people; and established institutions, accommodations and traditional practices."[15]

The secret of democracy is not that it seeks to build and develop good citizens or to mold character. Rather its strength lies in the development and cultivation of a political order that effectively protects different spheres of society. It does so, basically, by limiting its own powers through a variety of constitutional mechanisms (separation of powers,

---

[15]Goldwin, "Human Rights: The Moral Foundation," p. 8.

periodic elections, checks and balances, independent judiciary, etc.); the protection of social, cultural, and political pluralism; and the respect of an autonomous economy. Indeed, the existence of a vigorous scientific and educational community, private enterprise, and religious life all contribute to restraint and delimitation of governmental power. This is why pluralism and limited government are essential features of authentic democracy. The state is, of course, an important actor in national life, but it is not the sole or even most significant actor. And in a democratic nation, the sphere of the state is purposefully limited in order to allow other areas of life to be determined independently of government.

The Totalitarian Threat

The primary threat to human dignity in the contemporary world system is totalitarianism. By totalitarianism I mean the expansion of governmental power over significant aspects of human life, including social, political, economic, cultural, and religious dimensions.[16] Totalitarianism is a threat to human rights because it challenges the dignity of people by denying basic human freedoms, including the freedoms of religion and conscience. Indeed, the goal of modern totalitarianism is to replace religion with political ideology. John Courtney Murray observed that modern totalitarian systems were characterized by a "thorough-going monism of only one sovereign, one society, one law, and one faith."[17] He went on to point out that such monistic systems deny transcendence and seek to build an all-embracing state. The ruling party becomes the supreme spiritual, moral, and political authority.

The human costs of imposing a monistic political system are enormous. This has been especially the case with communism, the most brutal and destructive political system ever practiced on earth. It has been estimated that some 20 million people have perished in the Soviet Union alone; and

---

[16]Totalitarianism is a twentieth-century phenomenon. It could only have been practiced in a relatively modern, secular society, for only such a society has the communication, transportation, and social networks and the means by which a ruling political party can effectively influence and control human life.

[17]John Courtney Murray, quoted in Neuhaus, "Christianity and Democracy," p. 3.

the expansion of communism to China, Eastern Europe, and other areas of the world has resulted in as much human destruction. But the brutality of totalitarian communism is more than physical. As it has expanded, it has dwarfed human personalities; threatened culture, art, learning, and religion; and eliminated all significant social, political, and religious structures that are not supportive of the ruling party. The net result of the expansion of the Leninist monism in the Soviet Union and elsewhere is an incomprehensible human tragedy. It is important to recall that modern communist systems are the only regimes that fully regulate the emigration of citizens. The pain and destruction wrought by the Leninist machine is so great that the only way to contain the effects is to hermetically seal the state's territorial boundaries. On my second trip to the Soviet Union two years ago I asked a guide why there were so many guards at the border crossing, and she answered that they were there to control people trying to immigrate into the Soviet Union!

The brutal and expansionist foreign policies of communism need to be opposed. Christians need to be especially opposed to this political philosophy, for it is contrary to key elements of the Christian faith. The challenge posed by communism to Christianity is not political but moral. By seeking to extend the sphere of the state into all areas of life, including religion, it threatens life with a political monism incompatible with the Christian religion. It is impossible to reconcile the Leninist doctrine of political monism with dualism and transcendence of Christianity. Thus Christians must be unapologetically and fervently against communism. And to the extent that the Soviet Union is the prime bearer of the totalitarian philosophy, they must also oppose that political regime.

Since the mid 1970s there has been a growing conviction in some intellectual circles in the West that there is basically no moral difference between the United States and the Soviet Union. The belief in the moral symmetry between the two nations derives from the conviction that the two superpowers are both domestically imperfect and internationally militaristic and expansionistic. In a famous Oxford University debate on this topic in the early 1980s, historian E. P. Thompson, a leader in the European peace movement, argued that the United States and the Soviet Union were involved in an irrational military "quarrel" which propelled a military arms race. He asserted that both superpowers were politically expansionistic and similarly militaristic. There was, he suggested, a fundamental moral equivalence between the foreign policies of the United States and the Soviet Union. Indeed, Thompson argued that, if anything, the United States had been more irresponsible militarily in recent years than the Soviet Union.[18]

E. P. Thompson's approach to U.S.–Soviet relations is fundamentally flawed because it focuses exclusively on the military problem and denies distinctions between the political ideologies and social and economic structures of free and despotic societies. As Richard Neuhaus has observed, "More profound than the conflict of military and political forces, is the conflict over the dignity and destiny of the human person, and the societal order appropriate to that dignity and destiny."[19] By assuming the moral equivalence of the two superpower regimes, Thompson has neglected some of the most elemental moral distinctions in political life and has made the quest for human rights an absurdity. Former United Nations ambassador Jeane Kirkpatrick has observed:

> If it is no longer possible to distinguish between freedom and despotism—the U.S. is a free society; between consent and violence, we are a society based on consent; between open and closed societies, we are an open society—then the erosion of the foundation of a distinctively Western, democratic civilization is already far advanced and the situation is serious indeed.[20]

In addition to the myth of the moral equivalence of the superpowers, there is another widespread misconception about human rights violations—the myth of the equivalence of military dictatorships and communist governments, of authoritarian and totalitarian regimes. While all dictatorial regimes commit acts of repression and oppression, there is a fundamental philosophic distinction between totalitarianism and authoritarianism. The former seeks to impose a monistic

---

[18] Televised debate of the Oxford Union Debate between E. P. Thompson and Caspar Weinberger, U.S. Secretary of Defense, on the moral difference between the foreign policies of the United States and the Soviet Union, 1984. For a brief commentary on the debate, see L. Grafstein, "Oxford Diarist," *The New Republic,* April 2, 1984, p. 42.

[19] Neuhaus, "Christianity and Democracy," p. 10.

[20] Jeane Kirkpatrick, *Doctrine of Moral Equivalence,* U.S. Department of State, Bureau of Public Affairs, Current Policy No. 580, April 9, 1984, p. 6.

political order in society, while the latter seeks only the control of political power. This is why communism, the chief expression of totalitarianism in the world, is the major political doctrine challenging human rights in principle. Authoritarian regimes violate human rights, but when they do, they do so in the name of national security. As Senator Daniel Moynihan has noted, authoritarian governments "commit abominations in practice; the Communist countries commit abominations in principle."[21]

A military government can be brutal and oppressive, of course. The experience of military governments in Argentina, Chile, Brazil, and Uruguay in the 1970s documents this. But since such regimes are not monistic, they do not seek a monopoly of social, political, and economic control. Ambassador Kirkpatrick, who has called attention to the differences between authoritarian and totalitarian systems, has explained why military systems are less threatening to human rights than are communistic systems:

> Authoritarian governments are frequently corrupt, inefficient, arbitrary, and brutal, but they make limited claims on the lives, property, and loyalties of their citizens. Families, churches, businesses, independent schools and labor unions, fraternal lodges, and other institutions compete with government for loyalties and resources, and so limit its power. Authoritarian governments—traditional and modern—have many faults and one significant virtue: their power is limited and where the power of government is limited, the damage it can do is limited also. So is its duration in office. Authoritarian systems do not destroy all alternative power bases in a society. The persistence of dispersed economic and social power renders those regimes less repressive than a totalitarian system and provides the bases for their eventual transformation.[22]

That the evolution of democracy is more probable for authoritarian systems than totalitarian governments is documented by history: there is not one example of a country that has evolved from totalitarianism into democracy, while numerous authoritarian regimes (e.g., Argentina, Brazil,

---

[21]Daniel P. Moynihan, "The Politics of Human Rights," *Commentary*, Aug. 1977, p. 24.
[22]Jeane Kirkpatrick, "Human Rights and American Foreign Policy—A Symposium," *Commentary*, Nov. 1981, p. 44.

Peru, Portugal, Spain, and Venezuela) have experienced democratic transformations.

PROMOTING HUMAN DIGNITY

I have suggested that a moral foreign policy must affirm human dignity. Moreover, there is a legal responsibility to care for human rights abroad. For example, the United Nations charter affirms in its preamble "faith in fundamental human rights" and then specifies (in article 55) some of the human rights that the nations of the world should promote. The charter (in article 56) also requires that member states pledge themselves to take joint and separate action to promote such rights. The problem in foreign affairs is that the rights of states and the rights of people may come into conflict. This occurs when sovereign governments willfully and deliberately carry out policies that are an affront to human dignity. When this happens states have a moral obligation to assist peoples of other lands—to promote human dignity internationally—even if it involves encroachment on the political independence of other states. The principle of human justice must have an overriding priority over the claims of nonintervention and political independence, provided the international violations of rights are flagrant and well established.

In developing a moral human rights policy, it is important to identify states that flagrantly violate rights and devise credible strategies for promoting basic rights. Identifying states that commit gross human rights violations and impugn the dignity of people is not easy, especially since the most serious violations of basic rights are committed by closed societies. The mass genocide of some two million persons in Kampuchea, for example, did not become public knowledge until after the Khmer Rouge had been forced out of office.

There are two possible approaches in defining major human rights violations. The first approach is to identify violations on a case-by-case basis. There are numerous organizations, including the Department of State's Bureau of Human Rights and Amnesty International, which issue annual reports on human rights and thus identify and publicize human rights abuses. To a significant degree, the

United States government has relied in the past on this case-by-case identification of systematic rights violations. An alternative approach is to identify major categories of states that threaten human dignity. The aim here is to define the chief impediments to human dignity in order that a long-term human rights policy can be developed. The Reagan administration policy of defending democracy when it is threatened by external sources and promoting it where it does not exist is fundamentally based on this approach.

Table 5.1, which classifies nations in terms of political freedom and social and economic well-being, illustrates one possible way of identifying groups of states that threaten human dignity. The chart identifies two fundamental impediments to human dignity—political oppression and poverty. The alleviation of poverty will require increased economic productivity (a topic addressed in the following chapter), while the alleviation of political oppression will necessitate the establishment of free, constitutional governments. Although there is no simple blueprint for protecting the basic rights of people, I have suggested that democratic structures are the surest safeguard of basic rights. Democracies do, of course, violate human rights, but history suggests that they are much more prone to correct mistakes and evils than dictatorial or totalitarian regimes.

The group of nations that has the lowest living standards and the highest levels of political oppression (nations in the top, left square) represent nations in which human dignity is least honored. It would appear logical that the United States should focus attention on those regimes, but many of them are so backward that there is little likelihood that living conditions can be improved significantly. Moreover, political corruption is so rampant and governmental authority so diffuse that there is little chance for developing institutions that can effectively protect basic rights. The U.S. government can and should provide food and economic assistance to alleviate hunger and malnutrition in these nations, but there is little likelihood (because of limited absorptive capacities) that the underlying conditions in these nations can be reformed in the near future in order to significantly improve human rights and living conditions.

If the goal is to promote democracy, it is unlikely that such institutions can be promoted in the extremely backward nations of Africa or in nations that are already under the

Table 5.1
CLASSIFICATION OF NATIONS IN TERMS
OF POLITICAL WELL-BEING AND ECONOMIC WELL-BEING

Political Well-being

	NOT FREE	PARTLY FREE	FREE
OPPRESSIVE **PQLI: 1–40**	Afghanistan (17) Angola (27) Benin (38) Cntrl. Afr. Rep. (33) Chad (27) Ethiopia (31) Kampuchea (33) Mali (27) Mauritania (30) Mozambique (40) Niger (27) Oman (37) Pakistan (39) Somalia (17) Sudan (39)	Gambia (16) Ivory Coast (40) Nepal (30) Senegal (30) Sierra Leone (26) Yemen (26) (North)	
MINIMAL **PQLI: 47–79**	Algeria (50) China (PRC) (75) Congo (57) Ghana (48) Haiti (43) Libya (57) Namibia (50) Nigeria (41) Saudi Arabia (45) Zaire (51)	Brazil (74) El Salvador (69) Guatemala (60) Indonesia (58) Iran (57) Jordan (71) Kenya (56) Lebanon (77) Nicaragua (71) South Africa (68) Tunisia (65) Uganda (49) United Arab Em. (69) Zimbabwe (64)	Bolivia (53) Botswana (48) Dominican Rep. (70) Ecuador (73) Honduras (63) India (46) Papua New Guinea (45) Peru (69)

	NOT FREE	PARTLY FREE	FREE
SATISFACTORY PQLI: 80–100	Albania (82) Bulgaria (93) Cuba (95) Germany, Dem. Rep. (95) Romania (92) U.S.S.R. (94)	Chile (85) Granada (92) Mexico (80) Poland (94) Taiwan (92) Uruguay (90)	Argentina (89) Canada (97) Costa Rica (91) Denmark (98) Finland (98) France (98) Germany, Fed. Rep.(96) Japan (99) Iceland (100) Israel (92) Netherlands (98) Sweden (99) Switzerland (98) United Kingdom (96) U.S.A. (97) Venezuela (83)

Economic well-being is based here on the Physical Quality of Life Index (PQLI), which considers life expectancy at age one, infant mortality, and literacy. PQLI scores are in parentheses.

(Economic data from John W. Sewell, Richard E. Feinberg, and Valeriana Kallab, eds., *U.S. Foreign Policy and the Third World: Agenda 1985–86* [New Brunswick: Transaction Books], pp. 214–27. Political data from Raymond D. Gastil, *Freedom in the World: Political Rights and Civil Liberties 1984–1985* [Westport: Greenwood, 1985], p. 25.)

control of totalitarian communism. The choice of where democracy is promotable is much more limited. Samuel Huntington has suggested that the development of democracies occurs in nations that have a moderately well-developed social and economic structure. Accordingly, he suggests that if the United States wishes to promote democracy, it should concentrate its resources on states in the zone of transition— that is, moderately well-developed states whose traditional forms of government have become difficult to maintain in the light of increasing public demands and the evolution of a more complex social structure. According to him, the nations in this zone of transition include those in the upper middle-income group.[23] If Huntington's argument is valid, then the promotion of democracy should assist those relatively well-developed nations that are most susceptible to change. The irony of such a strategy is that the nations most open to democracy are those that are also more hospitable to human rights. Nations that violate human dignity the most are the least likely to improve human rights.

Strategy

The resources and opportunities available for promoting basic rights abroad are limited. It is therefore important to devise a modest strategy that responds to immediate crises as well as to the underlying conditions impeding human dignity. An effective strategy must have two distinct dimensions—a short-term focus on human rights violations and a long-term focus on the transformation of domestic structural impediments to human dignity.[24] The aim of the short-term approach is to respond to immediate political and economic crises. Such assistance might include, for example, massive economic relief to nations suffering from famine, such as Ethiopia and Chad in 1984 and 1985, or diplomatic and international pressures on states that are egregiously violating basic rights. The aim of the long-term approach is to advance the evolution of political and economic institutions and practices that are hospitable to human dignity. This

[23]Samuel P. Huntington, "Will More Countries Become Democratic?" *Political Science Quarterly*, vol. 99, no. 2 (Summer 1984), pp. 198–202.

[24]The Reagan administration's "dual-track" human rights policy has basically this dual short-term/long-term focus. For an explanation of this policy see the introduction of U.S. Department of State, *Country Reports on Human Rights for 1983* (Washington: GPO, 1984).

might be done through economic development programs and through political and military assistance in promoting democratic institutions and combating the spread of totalitarianism. I noted earlier that the major threat to human dignity in our contemporary world is communism. If the U.S. government is to bolster human dignity overseas, it is important to assist nations in protecting themselves from the forceful expansion of communism through military and political assistance. But impeding the expansion of communism is not enough. It is also essential to contribute positively to development of those underlying conditions on which democratic regimes can prosper. This will require political, economic, and, in some cases, military assistance. It is well-known that there are numerous social, cultural, and economic conditions generally associated with the expansion of democratic government. These include, among others, a prosperous market economy and a differentiated and pluralistic culture. To the extent possible the United States should assist nations in developing social, economic, and cultural structures conducive to democratic government.

One of the major problems in U.S. foreign policy is the determination of which countries should receive economic and military assistance and which should not. Since human rights violations are commonplace in developing nations, assistance to Third World governments will require an assessment of the government's protection of human dignity. U.S. government legislation requires that economic and military assistance may be given only to regimes that protect human rights.[25] Specifically, the Foreign Assistance Act of 1961 (section 116), as amended in 1976, prohibits economic aid to governments that engage in "a consistent pattern of gross violations of internationally recognized human rights," except where such assistance "will directly benefit the needy people in such country." The act (502B) also states that the president is to conduct the security assistance programs so as to "promote and advance human rights and avoid identification of the United States through such programs with governments which deny to their people internationally

---

[25] The Foreign Assistance Act defines human rights violations to include "torture or cruel, inhuman, or degrading treatment or punishment, prolonged detention without charges and trial, and other flagrant denials of the right to life, liberty or the security of the person."

recognized human rights and fundamental freedoms." The U.S. government, in short, can improve human rights only in those countries which are not themselves grossly violating human rights.

Principles

How should the United States promote human rights abroad? What norms should guide its conduct? I believe that an effective human rights policy must be guided by four general principles: a focus on actions and not words, an emphasis on the underlying social and political structures of society, an adherence to secret diplomacy, and a steadfastness to modesty of purpose.

The concern with actions and not rhetoric is important because of the tendency to politicize human rights and to focus on declarations and pronouncements rather than on performance. The achievement of rights does not depend on declarations or bills of rights, however, any more than dreams and ideals constitute reality. Declarations are not self-activating. Indeed, much harm can be done by focusing on public relations alone, since it can lead to a false reliance that distracts attention from the real dangers and the real remedies for human rights violations. Robert Goldwin has written that it is regrettable that so much time and energy has been devoted to the creation of the "cruel illusion" that asserting rights will somehow provide for more food. For example, Goldwin asserts that "it is either a conscious fraud, or a naïve faith in the magic of words to assert that recognizing the human right to enough food will resolve the problem. Whether fraud or folly, it is deplorable and shameful."[26] It is important, then, to recognize that laws, constitutions, pronouncements, and declarations do not themselves guarantee rights. Rights are protected and guaranteed by productive communities where the members choose to live by laws and rules. One of the great ironies of the human condition is that despicable tyrannies are often born of lofty ideals that become corrupted, twisted, and unrecognizable.

A second key principle is the cultivation of underlying

---

[26]Robert Goldwin, "Human Rights and American Foreign Policy, Part IV—Arguments and Afterwords," *The Center Magazine*, July–Aug. 1984, p. 59.

social and political conditions which sustain and preserve basic rights. A basic requirement for the protection and affirmation of rights is a well-constituted political and economic society. This truth is amply demonstrated by the historical evolution of Latin American governments. Many Latin American regimes have enacted provisions similar to those of the U.S. Constitution, yet few Latin American countries have successfully protected rights or operated in complete accord with their written constitutions. George F. Kennan, one of the most thoughtful students of foreign affairs, has observed that since human rights cannot be separated from the institutions and practices of government or the social and cultural institutions of a specific society, it is impossible to impose specific standards without corresponding changes in the other aspects of society on which those rights depend.[27] But since the development and evolution of a nation's social and political structures are a matter to be decided indigenously, influencing the evolution of the underlying social and political institutions is an exceedingly complex and difficult undertaking.

The third principle of a sound human rights policy is secret diplomacy. Historically, the more idealistic and moralistic American foreign policy has been, the greater the propensity to pursue foreign policy goals publicly and openly. Two presidents whose administrations were characterized by public diplomacy were Woodrow Wilson, a staunch Presbyterian who was committed in foreign affairs to the norm of "open covenants openly arrived at," and Jimmy Carter, who made human rights the centerpiece of his foreign policy. While public diplomacy can help influence world public opinion and can bring international pressure to bear on the policies and actions of government, it can also foster conflict among states and lead to counterproductive results. It is important not to forget that the basic legal norm of the existing world system is the sovereign independence of states. As Leonid Brezhnev once remarked, "to teach others how to live cannot be accepted by a sovereign state." If the United States is to challenge the sovereign actions and policies of other states, it should do so in the least threaten-

---

[27] George F. Kennan, "Ethics and Foreign Policy: An Approach to the Problem," in *Foreign Policy and Morality: Framework for a Moral Audit* (New York: Council on Religion and International Affairs, 1979), p. 44.

ing way. A quiet, secret human rights diplomacy may not encourage widespread domestic public support, but it will contribute more to the long-term promotion of human rights than an international public relations campaign. There is little evidence that the public diplomacy of President Carter contributed either to the human rights of Soviet Jews or to political opposition in Argentina, Chile, or Brazil. Indeed, the public criticism of the Pinochet regime in Chile seemed to have strengthened that government. To prove that he had public support for his policies, General Pinochet held a public referendum on his policies in 1978 and received more than 85 percent of the vote. As one Chilean citizen told me, "I don't like the policies of the military government, but I like the U.S. government's criticism even less." Given the sensitivity of human rights, a prudent foreign policy must necessarily be based on quiet, secret diplomacy.

A fourth principle is modesty of purpose. The effort to do good can lead to evil. We need to remember that moral indignation can corrupt. Since sin is universal and total, no person or nation can fully escape from evil and injustice. Human rights violations will persist until God himself establishes his kingdom on earth. In the meantime, however, Christians are called to promote human rights, but they must do so with modesty and sensitivity, recognizing that all human efforts are tainted with selfishness, including the efforts to promote the rights of other human beings. This is why Robert Goldwin has written that "whatever power is mustered to protect rights must be used in moderation, with restraint, under law, through constitutional institutions."[28] Even the efforts to combat evil political ideologies need to be constrained and limited lest the zeal to use power morally itself succumbs to immorality.

As leader of the free world, the United States can be proud of its national achievements and historical record. The principles of limited, constitutional government, along with the practice of free enterprise have resulted in a prosperous and political free society. But while the principles of democracy and private enterprise may be moral, the behavior of the United States is not. Our principles may be just, but we should not make the self-righteous mistake of confusing our principles with ourselves. The United States, as the chief

---

[28] Goldwin, "Human Rights: The Moral Foundation," p. 9.

bearer of the democratic alternative, has a special responsibility to promote human dignity. Richard Neuhaus has written eloquently of this responsibility:

> To say that America has a singular responsibility in this world historical moment does not mean that America is God's chosen nation, as for instance, Israel was chosen by God. God has made no special covenant with America as such. God's covenant is with his creation, with Israel, and with his Church. However, because America is a large and influential part of his creation, because America is the home of the heirs of Israel of old, and because this is a land in which his Church is vibrantly free to live and proclaim the Gospel to the world, we believe that America has a peculiar place in God's promises and purposes. This is not a statement of nationalistic hubris but an acknowledgement that we bear a particular and grave responsibility.[29]

[29]Neuhaus, "Christianity and Democracy," pp. 10–11.

6

REDUCING THIRD WORLD POVERTY

"U.S. citizens must demand a drastic reorientation of U.S. foreign policy. We must demand a foreign policy that unequivocally sides with the poor."

Ronald J. Sider[1]

"The United States can do much to help these peoples in their liberation. But we will not be true to our own preferences, or the promise of our system, if we divorce our policies toward the world's poor from the values, institutions, and international economic arrangements which we cherish for ourselves."

Nick Eberstadt[2]

One of the major problems of the contemporary world is the extreme poverty of most nations in Asia, Africa, and Latin America. In this chapter we will explore the nature of this world problem and examine what the United States can do to help alleviate basic human needs in the developing nations.

The problem of poverty is often defined in terms of income inequalities between the industrial nations of the

---

[1] Ronald J. Sider, *Rich Christians in an Age of Hunger* (Downers Grove: InterVarsity, 1977), p. 207.

[2] Nick Eberstadt, "Famine, Development & Foreign Aid," *Commentary*, March 1985, p. 31.

North and the Third World nations in the South. This chapter focuses, however, not on income inequalities between the rich and poor nations, but on the deplorable and inhuman conditions in which a large portion of the world's population lives. While the problems of world poverty and international economic inequality are closely related, they are conceptually distinct. The problem of international inequalities (addressed briefly in chapter 3) concerns economic disparities among states. It deals with the justice of the international economic order. The problem of world poverty, by contrast, is concerned with personal welfare, with the standard of living enjoyed by people. Its focus is human dignity, not equity. A reduction in the living standards of the rich can, of course, contribute to a short-term solution to the problem of poverty, just as the redistribution of national income can improve the lot of the poorest sectors within a society. But redistribution of income among or within states is an inadequate solution to the problem of poverty, especially if societies have a rapidly expanding population. British economist Brian Griffiths has written that "the redistribution of wealth is not an adequate solution to the problem of world poverty. Continued emphasis on redistribution can only exacerbate the world's economic problems."[3]

The creation of jobs is what is desperately needed in the Third World. Poor countries need to establish economic policies that foster job creation, and rich countries need to establish foreign economic policies that contribute to that task. If poverty is to be significantly reduced, the rich countries must assist the poorest Third World governments in undertaking programs that foster long-term wealth creation. Simple transfers of resources will not be sufficient, however. The record of the past thirty years clearly demonstrates this. The only viable solution for relieving massive poverty in developing nations is a cooperative venture between the rich industrial states and the poor nations themselves. Rich nations should, of course, provide immediate assistance to poor nations suffering from famine, earthquakes, or other similar disasters. But short-term assistance needs to be distinguished from the long-term programs of economic growth. The challenge in devising a moral interna-

---

[3] Brian Griffiths, *The Creation of Wealth* (London: Hodder and Stoughton), p. 13.

tional economic policy is how to help relieve short-term basic needs while also contributing to long-term economic development, which alone can provide a permanent solution to the needs of the poor.

THE NATURE OF POVERTY

While president of the World Bank, Robert McNamara coined the term *absolute poverty* to describe the condition of life so characterized by illiteracy, malnutrition, and disease as to be beneath any reasonable definition of decency. Estimates of the number of people living in this condition range from 500 million to 1.3 billion. In 1980, for example, the World Bank estimated that there were some 780 million persons in the Third World who were in this condition. The Overseas Development Council, which annually issues a report classifying countries on the basis of income statistics and other relevant socioeconomic indicators, identified thirty-nine countries (including China) with extreme poverty on the basis of 1982 data. According to Table 6.1, these thirty-nine countries had average per capita income of less than $250, a literacy rate of less than 40 percent, and a total population of 1.3 billion people. This group of states included twenty-seven African countries, eleven Asian countries, and one Latin American country. While use of comparative income statistics can result in highly misleading conclusions,[4] they call attention to the egregious income differences between the rich and poor countries and to the desperately low levels of living in some nations.

Social scientists disagree about the number of persons who suffer from hunger and malnutrition in the developing nations.[5] It is clear, however, that a major portion of the

---

[4]Comparative income statistics are misleading for three reasons: (1) the available quantitative data on developing nations is highly unreliable; (2) the data cannot be used comparatively because of different purchasing power and different living requirements (e.g., five dollars of earned income in, e.g., Haiti, has much greater relative value than the same income in a Western European nation); (3) income data underreports the productive activities of people, especially in the developing nations where a substantial portion of the productive enterprises are outside of the money economy.

[5]Some organizations, like the United Nations' Food and Agriculture Organization, estimate that the number of people lacking sufficient food is close to a half billion; others, such as Nick Eberstadt of Harvard University's Center for Population Studies, has suggested that a more realistic number is

Table 6.1
COMPARATIVE ECONOMIC AND
SOCIAL INDICATORS OF NATIONS

Country Classification	Per capita Income, 1982 (U.S. Dollars)	Population in 1984 (millions)	Literacy	PQLI*
Low-income (39)	$250	1,330	37	46
Lower Middle-Income (40)	$714	548.9	55	57
Upper Middle-Income (39)	$2,058	620.1	73	74
High-Income (52)	$9,364	1,183.9	97	95

*The Physical Quality of Life Index (PQLI) is based on life expectancy at age one, infant mortality, and literacy.

Source: John Sewell, Richard Feinberg, and Valeriana Kallab, eds., *U.S. Foreign Policy and the Third World: Agenda 1985–86* (New Brunswick: Transaction Books, 1985), p. 214.

world's 4.8 billion people live in conditions that are an affront to human dignity. Robert McNamara has observed that:

> hundreds of millions of people living in [developing nations] are caught up in conditions of deprivation that no set of statistics can begin to describe. The truth is that poverty in the developing world is an intolerable assault on human dignity and decency. Malnutrition, disease, illiteracy, unemployment and early death pervade these vast populations.[6]

For a large portion of the peoples in the low-income countries, life is, to use Thomas Hobbes's famous description of the state of nature, nasty, brutish, and short; and because

100 million. See his excellent and insightful study "Hunger and Ideology," *Commentary*, July 1981, pp. 40–49.

[6] Robert S. McNamara, *One Hundred Countries, Two Billion People* (New York: Praeger, 1973), p. 8.

this condition is an affront to our Creator, Christians must respond to it.

CHRISTIAN PERSPECTIVE ON WORLD POVERTY

The enormous poverty and human deprivation in the Third World presents a fundamental challenge to the church. Christians are called to affirm human dignity of all people, regardless of race, sex, or nationality. Because of the transcendent worth or sacredness of human beings, Christians must care for those in need. Publicly, this will involve participation in the development of government policies that promote human dignity domestically and internationally; privately, it will involve caring for the poor and the needy in one's neighborhood, state, or nation and contributing to associations and nonprofit organizations that distribute resources and alleviate hunger abroad.

Numerous biblical themes are relevant to the subject of economics in general and of world poverty in particular, but two are of special importance in dealing with the problem of Third World poverty—the biblical view of poverty and the mandate of creation.

The Bible and Poverty

Christians are called to demonstrate God's love to those in human need—the weak, the poor, the oppressed. Christians must care for those in need because God cares. This point, made repeatedly in the Scriptures, is most forcefully put by Jesus himself in his account of the Good Samaritan. According to Jesus, the Good Samaritan was the one who, unlike other more religious persons, responded directly to human needs. After suggesting that the person who demonstrated mercy and compassion was doing the will of the Father, Jesus said, "Go and do likewise" (Luke 10:37). On another occasion Jesus indicated that caring for the poor was a direct way of expressing love to the heavenly Father. He said: "I was hungry and you gave me something to eat, I was thirsty and you gave me something to drink, . . . I needed clothes and you clothed me. . . . I tell you the truth, whatever you did for one of the least of these brothers of mine, you did for me" (Matt. 25:35–40). Being Christlike means that we must care for the poor and show mercy to those in need, and we must do so not only because the poor need our assistance, but because assisting the poor provides a means by which God's redemptive love can be channeled through us.

The Scriptures also teach that people and nations who do not care for the needy will be judged harshly by the Creator. Moses, for example, spoke of God's economic accountability as follows: "Do not mistreat an alien or oppress him, for you were aliens in Egypt. Do not take advantage of a widow or an orphan. If you do and they cry out to me, I will certainly hear their cry. My anger will be aroused, and I will kill you with the sword; your wives will become widows and your children fatherless" (Exod. 22:21–24). The prophets Isaiah and Jeremiah repeatedly called attention to the importance of justice.

> Woe to those who make unjust laws,
>   to those who issue oppressive decrees,
> to deprive the poor of their rights
>   and withhold justice from the oppressed of my people,
> making widows their prey,
>   and robbing the fatherless.
> What will you do on the day of reckoning,
>   when disaster comes from afar?
>
> (Isa. 10:1–3)

> "Woe to him who builds his palace by unrighteousness,
>   his upper rooms by injustice,
> making his countrymen work for nothing,
>   not paying them for their labor."
>
> (Jer. 22:13–14)

And the prophet Amos similarly warned of the importance of concern for the poor, pleading, "Let justice roll on like a river" (Amos 5:24).

Some theologians have argued that God is biased in favor of the poor. Nicholas Wolterstorff, for example, has written:

> God is not on the side of Dutch-speaking people versus those who do not speak Dutch; on that he is even-handed. God is not on the side of football players versus those who do not play football; on that, too, he is even-handed. But the poor are different. It is against his will that there be a society in which some are poor; in his perfected Kingdom there will be none at all. It is even more against his will that there be a society in which some

are poor while others are rich. When that happens, then
he is on the side of the poor, for it is they, he says, who
are being wronged. He is not on the side of the rich, and
he is not even-handed.[7]

In 1986 the U.S. Catholic bishops issued a pastoral letter on
the U.S. economy. A primary assumption of the letter is a
preferential concern for the poor, both in the United States
and in the poor countries of the Third World. According to
the letter, biblical justice is to be measured by society's
treatment of the poor and the powerless. The bishops argue
that faithfulness to the Scriptures requires, among other
things, a compassion toward the weak and poor and the
"emptying of self" in order to experience the power of God.
Indeed, the letter suggests that the option for the poor is the
social and ecclesiological counterpart of the emptying of
Jesus in the Incarnation.[8]

While the Scriptures repeatedly express concern for the
poor and warn against the evils of wealth, the notion that
God is on the side of the poor is not the total biblical message
concerning wealth and poverty. God is the Maker and Ruler
of all peoples, groups, and nations. It is important to
recognize that God has the same loving concern for all
peoples and races and that he does not have nationalistic or
economic class preferences. He cares alike for the rich and
the poor, the Americans and the Soviets, the weak and the
powerful. It is unbiblical to hold that God is biased for poor
nations in Africa and Asia and against Western European
nations simply because the former are less economically
developed. As emphasized in chapter 2, God is a sovereign
God who judges nations in accordance with his standards of
justice. While God is not biased, the Scriptures warn of his
judgment against those who exploit the weak and the poor,
as well as against those who fail to care for those in need.
The biblical message thus involves God's universal love and
our responsibility to express that love to all, but especially to
those in need. "The sooner we move beyond the limiting
notion of God's bias toward the poor and the oppressed,"
writes Sam Portaro, Jr., "the more quickly we may recover

[7]Nicholas Wolterstorff, Until Justice and Peace Embrace (Grand Rapids:
Eerdmans, 1983), p. 76.
[8]U.S. Catholic Bishops, "Catholic Social Teaching and the U.S. Economy," Origins, vol. 16, no. 24 (Nov. 27, 1986), p. 418, art. 52.

the message of God's grace and love for us all—the affection of this impassioned and indiscriminant deity whose ways, thankfully, are not as ours."[9]

While the "preferential option" thesis has significant theological shortcomings, its chief limitation is the economic sociology on which it is based. When Wolterstorff writes that God is on the side of the poor because it is they who are being "wronged" in society, he is assuming that the creation of wealth is chiefly an enterprise in which the few exploit the many—the wealth of the rich is a by-product of the poverty of the poor. But is this an accurate explanation of how modern wealth is created? As I will argue below, most modern wealth derives from increased efficiency in production of goods and services. It is important, therefore, that when Christians articulate a biblical conception of poverty that they avoid simplistic and inaccurate assumptions about wealth creation.

The Mandate of Creation

One of the important themes of the Bible is the mandate of creation. After God created earth, he commanded man to rule over it. The biblical mandate of creation is rooted in the fact that human beings are created in the image of God. Unlike animals, people have the unique capacity of acting morally, of deciding right from wrong. Their responsibility in managing and controlling the physical world derives from the special place that they have in the created order. Pope John Paul II in his encyclical *Laborem Exercens* observes that "man is the image of God partly through the mandate received from his Creator to subdue, to dominate, the earth. In carrying out this mandate, man, every human being, reflects the very action of the Creator of the universe."[10]

The ultimate purpose for human work is not to acquire possessions for ourselves, but to fulfill the biblical mandate to create. We are called to work because this is what God wants us to do—to subdue and dominate the earth. God's work of creation is not complete. Indeed, God uses humans to continue his redemptive work. Work also becomes the vehicle for self-realization and self-expression. Work, in

[9]Sam A. Portaro, Jr., "Is God Prejudiced in Favor of the Poor?" *The Christian Century*, April 24, 1985, p. 405.

[10]Pope John Paul II, *Laborem Exercens [On Human Work]*, 1981, p. 4.

other words, provides a means by which God's creativity can be expressed in and through us. *Toward the Future*, a study of the U.S. economy by Catholic lay leaders, expresses the divine character of work well:

> Creation is not finished. Much of use to humans remains hidden within it. Humans become co-creators through discovery and invention, following the clues left by God. Yet human beings are creators not only in changing the world, but also in realizing their own inner possibilities. Every human being who works must be respected as a person.[11]

Since the earth belongs to God, the acquisition and use of resources are ultimately accountable to God—the Creator, Sustainer, and Owner of the world. The purpose for work is not to increase possessions by which life can be more secure; rather the biblical aim of work is to provide a means of service to God and to other human beings. British economist Brian Griffiths has provided a thoughtful description of the biblical view of work:

> Man has been created with an urge to control and harness the resources of nature in the interests of the common good, but he is subject to his accountability to God as trustee to preserve and care for it. This process is precisely what an economist would refer to as a responsible form of wealth creation. Anything which transforms the material world so that it can be of greater use to fellow human beings is an act of wealth creation.[12]

Our brief summary of biblical perspectives does not provide a complete perspective of the biblical view of wealth and poverty, but it provides two essential clues to a Christian approach to Third World poverty. First, a Christian approach must seek to encourage the expansion of employment opportunities and to increase the productive levels of existing jobs. Since human labor is a divine mandate, a responsible foreign policy must seek to create jobs where there is massive unemployment or underemployment, as is the case in most Third World nations. Second, a Christian approach must be sensitive to the needs of the poor and

---

[11]The Lay Commission on Catholic Social Teaching and the U.S. Economy, *Toward the Future* (New York: American Catholic Committee, 1984), pp. 25–26.

[12]Griffiths, *Creation of Wealth*, p. 52.

dispossessed. The rampant poverty, malnutrition, and illness of the developing nations is an affront to the Creator. In responding to those in need, Christians fulfill the divine mandate of love.

SOURCES OF THIRD WORLD POVERTY

If the U.S. government is to help alleviate basic human needs in the Third World, it will have to devise policies that promote the creation of jobs and remove the underlying sources of poverty. Before examining the underlying conditions facilitating wealth creation, it is important to critique a highly popular but erroneous explanation of Third World poverty. This explanation, which we shall call the structural thesis, places blame for the world's poverty on the West and, more specifically, on the contemporary international economic structures.

The structural thesis attributes Third World poverty to the international economic institutions and especially to the policies of the United States and other developed nations. According to this perspective, the contemporary international economy is essentially capitalistic and is responsible for the uneven and unjust development of the world. The reason for the substantial income inequalities between the rich and poor nations is that the former have used their political and economic power to exploit the Third World. In the nineteenth and early twentieth centuries rich states dominated the poor nations through colonialism; domination is now alleged to be maintained through multinational corporations and the institutions of the world economy (e.g., the International Monetary Fund, World Bank, and trade policies).

The structural thesis is appealing because it is simple and because it externalizes the causes of poverty. However simple and appealing this perspective may be, it is wholly inadequate as an explanation for Third World poverty. To be sure, exploitation has not been confined to capitalist economies or to states participating in international trade. The claim that the reform of domestic and international economic structures automatically leads to social justice is wholly unwarranted and is based on two fallacious assumptions common to the structuralist perspective.

First, the creation of wealth is assumed to be the result

of exploitation. This fallacious assumption derives from the idea that the gains of the rich countries come at the expense of the poor nations and peoples. Nicholas Wolterstorff, for example, in *Until Justice and Peace Embrace*, argues that the poverty of the Third World is a direct result of the capitalistic growth of the West. Wolterstorff writes:

> It is now clear that the mass poverty is not the normal situation of mankind, nor is it the consequence of the actions of a few aberrant individuals. It is in good measure the effect of our world-wide economic system and of the political structures that support it.[13]

Capitalist growth may breed income inequality, especially in the early stages of economic development as it rewards peoples, groups, and nations that are most productive. This expansion does not come through exploitation; it comes through increases in productivity which derive not from finding new resources but from more efficient production and distribution of goods and services. This is why the lay Catholic study *Toward the Future*, issued as a complementary analysis to the bishops' pastoral letter on the U.S. economy, questions the view that the creation of wealth is necessarily exploitative. The lay letter says that the notion that the wealth of some states causes the poverty of others is empirically unfounded. "We reject as false," reads the report, "the proposition that the poverty of poor nations is caused by the wealth of richer nations."[14] Economist Brian Griffiths has similarly called into question the exploitation thesis:

> In general terms it is impossible to accept the thesis that the poverty of the Third World is the result of the prosperity of the First World. The Third World has certain legitimate grievances against the First World but at best these are marginal in explaining Third World poverty. What is not generally recognized is that the currently fashionable quasi-Marxist framework within which Third World problems are being analyzed is counter productive to the real plight of the distressed in these countries. It is counter productive because it has resulted in the whole-

---

[13] Wolterstorff, *Until Justice*, p. 97.
[14] Lay Commission on Catholic Social Teaching and the U.S. Economy, *Toward the Future*, p. 50. For a different point of view see Ronald Mueller, "Poverty Is the Product," *Foreign Policy* 13 (Winter 1973–74).

sale politicisation of the issues involved. The major issue of poverty has been changed very subtly to a discussion of inequality, the focus is on groups, classes and nations but rarely the plight of the individuals; the material is emphasized to the [ex]clusion of the immaterial, the causes of poverty are external factors but rarely home grown, and finally the responsibility is shifted from individuals to governments. Put bluntly, it totally distorts and undermines a Christian perspective on global poverty.[15]

A second erroneous assumption is the belief that the gains from trade between rich and poor nations accrue inexorably to the rich. Ronald Sider in *Rich Christians in an Age of Hunger* observes that:

> We are all implicated in structural evil. International trade patterns are unjust. An affluent minority devours most of the earth's non-renewable natural resources. Food consumption patterns are grossly lopsided. And the returns on investment in poor countries are unjustly high. Every person in developed countries benefits from these structural injustices. Unless you have retreated to some isolated valley and grow or make everything you use, you participate in unjust structures which contribute directly to the hunger of a billion malnourished neighbours.[16]

Empirical data do not corroborate Sider's simplistic conclusion. Trade is not the cause of poverty; otherwise countries such as Japan, Saudi Arabia, and Taiwan would not have developed economically in the postwar years. Nor can the economic backwardness of the poor nations be explained by their contact with rich countries. Colonialism, as British economist P. T. Bauer has noted, cannot explain the poverty of Asia and Africa.[17] There are many poor countries that were never colonies (e.g., Afghanistan, Liberia, Nepal, and Tibet), while there are many colonies that have achieved a significant standard of living (e.g., Singapore and Hong Kong). Lester Thurow has said, "All our historical evidence indicates that it costs a country more to maintain an empire than it gains from having an empire. That was true in the

[15] Brian Griffiths, *Morality and the Market Place* (London: Hodder and Stoughton, 1982), p. 136.

[16] Sider, *Rich Christians*, p. 162.

[17] P. T. Bauer, *Dissent on Development* (Cambridge: Harvard University Press, 1972), pp. 150–63.

days of nineteenth century colonialism . . . and it is just as true today."[18]

Similarly, the poverty of Third World states cannot be explained by the existence of multinational corporations. Contact with the North through foreign direct investment has not led to a decline in living standards.[19] Although foreign investment has contributed to income inequalities domestically and internationally, it has provided the means by which to lift people out of backwardness and misery. Professor P. T. Bauer has carefully analyzed the economic growth patterns of developing nations and has concluded that the North has been a major contributor to the economic development of the South. He says:

> So far from the West having caused the poverty of the Third World, contact with the West has been the principal agent of material progress there. Indeed, the very idea of material progress is Western, especially in the sense of a constant and steadily increasing control over man's environment.[20]

In the last analysis, the structuralist thesis is an inadequate explanation of poverty because it underestimates the problems of economic production. Throughout most recorded history, the dominant human condition has been poverty and scarcity. The dramatic improvement in the standards of living in the twentieth century have not been an automatic by-product of economic life, but the consequence

---

[18]Lester Thurow, "The Arms Race and the Economic Order," in Philip J. Murnion, ed., *Catholics and Nuclear War* (New York: Crossroad, 1983), p. 207.

[19]See Robert W. Jackman, "Dependence on Foreign Investment and Economic Growth in the Third World," *World Politics* 34 (Jan. 1982): 175–97. Jackman argues, among other things, that the expansion of foreign investment spreads economic growth. There has been considerable debate about the relationship of growth to equity. Some have argued that the results of economic growth have had an absolute negative effect. This view has generally been based on the relative distribution of income, not on the absolute incomes of different social groups. In a significant case study on Brazil, Gary Fields showed that, contrary to the widely held belief that the poor people had been made worse off during the economic expansion of that nation, the poor in Brazil "did benefit from the economic growth that took place during the 1960s." See Gary S. Fields, "Assessing Progress Toward Greater Equality of Income Distribution," in *The Gap Between Rich and Poor*, ed. Mitchell A. Seligson (Boulder: Westview, 1984), pp. 292–320.

[20]P. T. Bauer, "Western Guilt and Third World Poverty," *Commentary*, Jan. 1976, p. 22.

of specific social, political, and economic developments associated with modernization. The structuralist perspective does not explain the creation of wealth. It simply attributes inequalities of income to international exploitation. Before resources can be distributed, they must be produced. What is significant about the modern era is the dramatic rise in world income, making possible enormous improvements in living conditions worldwide. People are better off today than they were at the turn of the century. As Barbara Ward has noted, the idea that most people can have access to a little modest affluence is a wholly new development in the history of civilization.[21] If the abject poverty of the developing nations is to be reduced, it will require more than the transfer of food and material resources. Giving food and other essential goods may respond to the immediate needs, but teaching people how to increase production will be the only viable long-term solution. Thus, if the United States is to help reduce Third World poverty, it must devise a long-term strategy designed to promote economic growth through job creation.

THE CREATION OF WEALTH

I observed earlier that there were radical disparities in living standards among the world's nations. Why are the disparities so great? What explains the wealth of some nations and the poverty of others? Is wealth the natural condition of life and poverty some temporary aberration inflicted by external forces? Or is wealth a result of deliberate human efforts? What are the personal attributes and societal elements associated with wealth creation? It is beyond the scope of this study to explore these questions in any depth, but if we are to illuminate a path which is to contribute to the well-being of Third World peoples, we will have to be guided by principles that adequately explain how wealth has been created in the modern world.

At the sake of oversimplification, let me list four basic ideas that explain the economic expansion of the West:

1. The basic condition of human civilization has been poverty.

---

[21] Barbara Ward, *The Rich Nations and the Poor Nations* (New York: Norton, 1962), pp. 22–27.

2. The reduction of poverty (expansion of wealth) is the result of increased productivity. The rise of human production makes improved levels of living possible.
3. Increased productivity is fundamentally explained by noneconomic factors. The primary determinants of wealth creation are human, not physical, resources.
4. Increased productivity is associated with modernization which, in turn, is facilitated by favorable cultural, social, political, and economic developments.

Of these four ideas, the last two are the ones that have been most frequently challenged, implicitly and explicitly, within the context of the problem of Third World poverty. It is important, therefore, to explain them further.

According to P. T. Bauer, economic achievement depends primarily on people's abilities and attitudes as well as on the society's social and political climate. "Differences in these determinants or factors," he notes, "largely explain differences in levels of economic achievement and rates of material progress."[22] The underlying conditions of development are not financial or material resources, but the human qualities that promote productivity.

But human qualities are not often emphasized in Third World development programs. Roger Darling, a former U.S. Agency for International Development official, has observed that the equating of development with resources is perhaps the most prevalent misconception about development.[23] This misconception is so widespread that the division of the world into rich and poor countries is based on readily quantifiable resources and conditions, while programs designed to improve the quality of life in the poor countries are similarly defined in terms of improvements in social and economic indicators.

It is often suggested that the wealth of the developed industrial nations is explained by the availability of primary resources. But resource disparities do not themselves explain the poverty and wealth of nations. Indeed, the focus on tangible economic resources is misplaced, for the creation of wealth has little to do with the availability of basic economic products and resources. Economic expansion may have been

---

[22] Bauer, Western Guilt, p. 75.
[23] Roger Darling, How Humanitarianism Impedes Third World Development (Vienna, Va.: Lectures-Seminars).

generated in ancient and medieval times by access to physical resources, but this is most assuredly not the case now. In fact, Max Singer and Paul Bracken have observed that modern wealth is not based on finding resources, but on creating new goods and services or producing goods more efficiently. Indeed, modern wealth is not based on things at all, they argue, but on ideas, techniques, information, and other intangibles that encourage higher productivity through better motivation, superior organization, and more efficient marketing.[24] The truth of this assertion is corroborated by the modern economic history of many developed nations, including Germany, Hong Kong, Singapore, and Switzerland, all of which have limited physical resources but have achieved impressive standards of living.

The human qualities on which wealth creation rests do not appear in a vacuum. Rather, they are nourished and protected in a particular environment in which the culture and political and economic institutions are conducive to economic enterprise. Typically, this environment requires an increasing level of modernization—a term used to denote social values and institutions associated with the promotion of material progress as well as the process by which societies become more secular, differentiated, and future-oriented. Since modernization is the means by which peoples and nations gain greater control over the social and economic environment, it is an inescapable element in the expansion of national wealth.

Brian Griffiths has suggested that one of the primary determinants of wealth creation is a culture conducive to investment.[25] The Catholic lay report referred to earlier also calls attention to the environmental elements that facilitate and inhibit economic development. According to the study, the two primary elements affecting productivity are culture (the habits, skills, attitudes, values, and morals of people) and the institutions of political economy (the prevailing systems of government and economic activity).[26]

Michael Novak has similarly written of the decisive role of religious and cultural norms in the expansion of a nation's

[24]Max Singer and Paul Bracken, "Don't Blame the U.S.," *New York Times Magazine*, Nov. 7, 1976, p. 34.
[25]Griffiths, *Creation of Wealth*, pp. 31–34.
[26]Lay Commission on Catholic Social Teaching and the U.S. Economy, *Toward the Future*, p. 47.

economic production. According to Novak, the reason for this is that these norms—or what he calls "the moral cultural system"—determine the institutions and practices of political economy. Novak illustrates the importance of culture by comparing the economic histories of two regions—Latin America and the United States. According to him, in the mid nineteenth century, the levels of economic development were roughly the same in North and South America, but during the next one hundred years the United States developed significantly while Latin American economies remained nearly static. Novak's explanation for the different paths in economic development is simple: "Latin Americans do not value the same moral qualities North Americans do. The two cultures see the world quite differently."[27] If the cultural norm and institutions of political economy are as significant as they are alleged to be, the only way of promoting long-term growth is through the nurturing of values and institutions conducive to wealth creation. This is why Griffiths says that while all cultures need to be respected, "they do not all deserve equal protection and promotion."[28]

The Role of Modernization

The expansion of modernization throughout the world has not resulted in immediate and always beneficial consequences. One of the sorrows of the modern world is that, while the beneficence of modern science and technology has contributed immensely to the well-being of people throughout the world, it has also resulted in enormous misery. The reason for these contradictory outcomes lies in the different patterns of economic development. Whereas modern values and institutions evolved over several centuries in the developed nations of North America and Western Europe, most advancing nations were thrust into the modern age in one brief period of time. This radical shift from an agrarian culture to an urban-oriented society has left profound consequences on the people of Africa, Asia, and Latin America. As a result of this sudden radical transformation in

---

[27]Michael Novak, *The Spirit of Democratic Capitalism* (New York: Simon and Schuster, 1982), p. 302.
[28]Griffiths, *Morality*, p. 143.

values and institutions, the people of the Third World have experienced traumatic physical and psychological consequences, much like a child being tossed into an adult workplace.

One of the most significant and fateful differences between rich and poor nations is that in the former, modern medicine was introduced at the time that modern economic institutions and practices had already come into being. But this was not the case in the Third World, where modern medicine was introduced prior to the development of viable economic and social systems. The result of this unbalanced expansion of modernization has been a dramatic decline in the death rate, resulting in a population explosion. Fundamentally, the population explosion is the result of the application of modern medicine to the underdeveloped areas of the world. From 1960 to 1978, for example, the thirty-eight poorest nations of the world decreased their crude death rate from twenty-four to fifteen per thousand, while the life expectancy rate for the same states rose from an average (weighted) of forty-two to fifty years. While beneficial, these developments have contributed to a population explosion which has exacerbated poverty and malnutrition.

The population explosion is significant because it creates severe social dislocations and places enormous strains on the social and political systems of nations. For example, Mexico's population growth rate during the past two decades has been close to 3 percent per year, and this has led to an unstable demographic distribution, with nearly 50 percent of its population now under the age of fifteen. But a rapid growth rate not only has potential damaging social and political effects, it has immediate economic results: it lowers the average income of all citizens. A nation with a 3 percent population growth rate must expand economically at 3 percent simply to maintain living conditions. While average population growth rates have begun to decline in most regions, Robert McNamara has cautioned that the Third World population growth rates still remain a "time bomb."[29]

---

[29]See Robert McNamara, "Time Bomb or Myth: The Population Problem," *Foreign Affairs*, Summer 1984, pp. 1107–31. McNamara suggests that while there have been appreciable declines in population growth rates in some Third World countries, there are nearly 1.1 billion people in developing nations, where there has been no appreciable decline in the fertility rate. Unless fertility changes in countries such as India and Bangladesh, their

The Third World's hunger and dismal living standards are not new events in human history. What is new is the scope of the problems at a time of unprecedented productive potential. Our challenge is to harness the forces of modernity that have made possible the unparalleled improvement in living standards and apply them to poor countries. At a general level the problem of poverty is the result of uneven and insufficient modernization. A more penetrating program of economic expansion is needed. If hunger and absolute poverty are to be reduced in the Third World, more jobs will have to be created.[30]

Our brief examination of the causes of Third World poverty has called into question the prevalent theory attributing hunger and poverty to the economic expansion of the West. I have indicated that the causes of contemporary world poverty are rooted in the underlying cultural and moral systems of developing nations and in the incomplete and disjointed application of modernity in those states. If U.S. foreign policy is to help reduce Third World poverty, it will have to contribute to the balanced expansion of modernization and the evolution of cultural patterns and economic and political institutions conducive to growth. The United States can and should provide resources for people suffering from absolute hunger, but it also should promote ideals and institutions that contribute to political freedom and economic expansion. The United States does not have a right to tell other states how to live, but it does have a moral responsibility to assist those in need and to teach others how to create wealth.

THE U.S. GOVERNMENT
AND THIRD WORLD POVERTY

I have proposed that Christians bear a dual mandate to care for the poor and to be productive through human labor.

population will undoubtedly double over the next forty-five years, resulting in an increase of nearly 600 million people in India and 150 million in Bangladesh.

[30] In 1985 the International Labor Organization estimated that nearly 1 billion jobs would need to be created by the year 2000 if the rates of unemployment are to be significantly reduced and jobs provided for those entering the work force. See *The Christian Science Monitor*, Aug. 30, 1985, pp. 1, 7.

My analysis of Third World poverty has also pointed out that the most effective way by which Christians can contribute to the long-term alleviation of Third World poverty is to promote employment abroad. Caring for the poor and fulfilling the creation mandate are thus two closely linked elements.

Developing an effective U.S. foreign economic policy will require the full integration of these two mandates, for the moral responsibilities of government are not identical to those of individuals. Whereas individuals are called to love and care for neighbors, governments are called to be just— that is, to distribute scarce resources fairly among different peoples and nations and among different generational groups. While individuals have a responsibility to care for the immediate needs of the poor, governments must respond equitably to a multitude of claims, weighing and assessing the merits of alternative decisions.

The Case for Foreign Aid

Numerous reasons have been set forth for giving foreign aid. The most compelling reason why the U.S. government should assist the people of the Third World is the moral or humanitarian justification. For example, one popular justification for aid is that it promotes political stability and democracy; another is that it contributes to the prosperity of both recipient and donor states. This latter view, expressed by the Brandt Commission Report,[31] assumes that what is good for the Third World is good for the United States and vice-versa. Still another rationale for aid is that it rectifies past exploitation. This justification—known as the "reparations thesis"—assumes that the West has exploited the Third World in the past and, now that the West is rich, it has an obligation to repay the developing nations for wealth that was unjustly extracted from them. The problem with these latter justifications is that they are morally and empirically weak.

Foreign assistance cannot guarantee friendship, cannot ensure the development of political stability, and cannot ensure mutual economic development. Foreign aid can,

[31] Report of the Independent Commission on International Development Issues, *North-South: A Programme for Survival* (Cambridge: MIT Press, 1980), pp. 20–23.

however, be an effective means for demonstrating a moral concern to people in need. According to the humanitarian justification, nations that have been blessed materially should give aid to those suffering from absolute poverty. The reason why assistance should be given is moral, not political, strategic, or economic. Individuals and the United States as a nation must give to those in need because it is right for them to do so. This view, which has always been included among the official justifications of U.S. assistance, was expressed by Cyrus Vance while serving as secretary of state:

> Our foreign policy flows from what we are as a people— our history, our culture, our values, and our beliefs. One reason this nation has a foreign aid program is that we believe we have a humanitarian and moral obligation to help alleviate poverty and promote more equitable economic growth in the developing world. We cannot be indifferent when half a billion people are hungry and malnourished, when 700 million adults are illiterate, and when one and a half billion people do not have minimal health care. As a free people who have achieved one of the highest standards of living in the world, we cannot fail to respond to such staggering statistics and the individual lives they encompass. We can be proud that we are a people who believe in the development of human potential.[32]

If the United States bears a moral responsibility to care for those in need, there is much less certainty about how much and through what channels such assistance should be given. For example, should the United States give aid to all people who have needs or only to those suffering from disasters and famine? To whom should aid be given—to the people directly or to governments? Should aid be transferred directly by U.S. government agencies or indirectly through multilateral institutions? Should the government rely primarily on private agencies or public organizations to distribute financial resources? Most importantly, should the financial assistance to the Third World be primarily for famine relief or for economic development? We shall attempt to answer some of these questions by analyzing policies which might

---

[32]Cyrus Vance, "Foreign Assistance and U.S. Policy," *Department of State Bulletin*, June 1978, p. 14.

contribute to the improvement of living standards in the developing nations.

The Nature of Aid

In considering the role of economic aid in the alleviation of Third World poverty, it is important to differentiate between short-term relief aid and longer-term development aid. The purpose of humanitarian aid is to alleviate short-run basic human needs resulting from disasters, famine, or civil strife; development aid, by contrast, is designed for improving economic production either through infrastructure expansion or through modernization of productive resources. The former provides food, medicine, clothing, and the like to meet immediate human needs; the latter involves the transfer of credit, capital, and technology in order to develop the productive capacities of nations.

There can be little doubt that the biblical model of the Good Samaritan places a direct moral responsibility not only on individuals, but also on materially blessed societies to respond to human suffering, especially that caused by unexpected disasters. Whether given through public or private channels, people bear a moral responsibility to care for those who suffer. While there is a clear and compelling moral justification for humanitarian aid, the rationale for development assistance is much more ambiguous. Since the aim of such assistance is to promote job creation, whether or not such assistance should be provided, and through what institutions, will depend not so much on the theology of the Sermon on the Mount as on the political economy of development. What is important in devising a prudent foreign economic policy is to assess the probable consequences of alternative public policies.

POLICY RECOMMENDATIONS

1. Increase the Level of Assistance

The U.S. government has historically been generous toward the needs of other nations. The total U.S. foreign economic assistance from 1945 until 1983 was $137.8 billion.[33] Of this amount more than 80 percent was direct

---

[33] Agency for International Development, U.S. Overseas Loans and Grants, Obligations and Loan Authorizations, July 1, 1945–Sept. 30, 1983, p. 4.

financial assistance to the Third World. In 1985 total U.S. foreign economic assistance was about $9 billion. Among the developed nations, the United States is the largest donor of economic aid, contributing about 20 percent of all net official assistance. Regrettably, the United States contributes one of the smallest proportions of aid of any of the Western developed states. Whereas most Western European nations contribute at least .5 percent of their gross national product, the United States contributes about .25 percent of its gross national product. In the light of the major needs of the world, the U.S. government can and should do more.[34]

Obviously, increases in aid should be distributed with care to ensure that it benefits people in greatest need. Private organizations should be increasingly used to channel this additional aid, for they have proven to be remarkably effective in directing resources to those suffering from absolute poverty. The strengthening of private associations and religious organizations concerned with medical, educational, nutritional, and economic needs of the developing nations would be an important way by which the U.S. government could direct additional resources to those in greatest need.

2. Reduce Direct Aid to Governments

Most development aid is given to governments. This is unfortunate, for many Third World governments are a major cause of poverty and an impediment to the improvement of living conditions for the poorest peoples. Since most Third World countries are nondemocratic and nonpluralistic, the resource transfers increase the influence of ruling, authoritarian elites. Moreover, since corruption is a major problem in developing nations, the transfer of funds to rulers and bureaucrats tends to further corruption in the developing nations. The misallocation of resources is also facilitated by official transfers, since investment decisions become based more on political criteria than on economic merit. Economic aid to governments is also detrimental in that it further centralizes economic decision making. Because developing nations rely extensively on central planning, official aid has

---

[34] For an excellent source on comparisons of foreign economic assistance, see the appendices in John W. Sewell, Richard Feinberg, and Valeriana Kallab, eds., *U.S. Foreign Policy and the Third World: Agenda 1985–86* (New Brunswick: Transaction Books, 1985), pp. 201–11.

further strengthened the practice of planning, which has yet to demonstrate its effectiveness in wealth creation. Economic aid transfers can also be detrimental in that they increase the politicization of life, strengthening already powerful regimes. Finally and most significantly, the poorest people are seldom the real beneficiaries of official aid. P. T. Bauer, who has devoted much of his professional life to the analysis of the role of aid in economic development, writes:

> Official aid does not go to the poor people, to the skeletal figures of aid propaganda. It goes instead to their rulers whose spending policies are determined by their own personal and political interests, among which the position of the poorest has very low priority. Indeed, to support rulers on the basis of the poverty of their subjects is more likely to encourage policies of impoverishment than to deter them.[35]

In short, the Third World nations need the assistance of the developed nations, but such aid, if it is to reach those in absolute poverty, must be channeled through private or multilateral institutions. Direct government to government loans and grants should be minimized.

3. Emphasize Nonresource Transfers

As noted previously, one of the widespread misconceptions associated with aid programs is that development and resource accumulation are synonymous. Resource transfers can, of course, contribute to economic expansion, but the basic ingredients of wealth creation are intangible human qualities, not tangible resources such as equipment, credits, raw materials, or new technology. The truth of this conclusion is borne out in our families. If we consider the development of children, for example, their own maturation results not so much from gifts from parents as from the development of self-discipline, persistence, and human learning skills. But resource transfers do not lead to development. The Marshall Plan was an effective economic assistance program not because of the magnitude of American aid, but because the assistance was provided to countries where human capital was well developed. The Marshall Plan

---

[35] P. T. Bauer, *Equality, The Third World and Economic Delusion* (Cambridge: Harvard University Press, 1981), p. 111.

did not start a program of development, but provided the tools to implement well-developed human capabilities.

One of the reasons why aid programs have focused on tangible resources is that it is easier to transfer resources than to promote the development of intangible human qualities. If economic potential of nations is to be enhanced, however, the United States needs to emphasize the development of human skills and attitudes, without which there can be no increase in productivity. Organizations like the Peace Corps that emphasize education and human development can contribute greatly to the acquisition of skills, knowledge, and attitudes essential to job creation. There is a great need for Americans who can educate and train the poor people of developing regions.

4. *Strengthen Aid Accountability*

A common by-product of foreign aid is that it encourages waste and mismanagement and results in the misallocation of scarce resources. The goal of development aid, of course, is to increase the productive capacities of states, but this has not always occurred. Indeed, foreign aid has delayed needed domestic reforms, channeled resources into wasteful investments, and inhibited the creation of an environmental climate conducive to investment.

The current foreign debt problem of many Third World nations illustrates the potential mismanagement possible through foreign assistance. In 1984 the total external public debt of non-oil developing nations exceeded $700 billion. The annual debt service for such loans was nearly $110 billion, with many nations spending more than 50 percent of their foreign exchange just on loan interest. The aim of Western economic assistance has been to increase Third World capital in order to increase productivity, but loans have not been wisely invested, and many poor nations have been unable to repay not only the principal, but also the periodic interest payments.

The mismanagement of foreign aid is especially evident in Africa, a continent where in 1985 more than 150 million people were on the verge of starvation. During the 1960s and 1970s the West provided significant economic assistance to African nations, but these resources, with few exceptions, contributed little to the productive capacities of the region. For example, during the 1960–83 period, Africa's external debt increased nearly tenfold (from $5.7 billion to $51.3 billion), while in the 1970s the sub-Saharan nations, the region most affected by hunger at this time, received more than $22 billion in aid.[36] Notwithstanding the major infusions of Western capital into agricultural projects, African per capita agricultural production actually declined from the mid 1970s to the mid 1980s.

The transfer of aid can result in harmful consequences, however. These include corruption, price distortions inhibiting domestic production, and politicization of production and distribution of goods and services. For example, while U.S. agricultural transfers (through P.L. 480) provide much-needed grains and foodstuffs to people suffering from hunger, such aid is also harmful in that it depresses food prices and thereby reduces agricultural production, which in turn makes a poor country even more dependent on rich nations. It is one thing to give disaster relief to people suffering from climatic catastrophes; it is quite another matter to give food on a continuing basis to an overpopulated poor nation. When this pattern occurs governments can continue unproductive economic policies and delay the difficult adjustments required to effectively cope with the social imbalances in agricultural demand and supply. In granting aid the challenge is to provide help that will alleviate short-term needs without creating conditions that impede the development and evolution of a framework conducive to economic growth.

According to Garrett Hardin, a scientist who has advocated an ethic of "tough love" toward the Third World,[37] in 1950 both China and India were poor and suffering from severe hunger, but during the postwar years both states pursued different social policies which have resulted in different levels of economic production. China refused to depend on outside resources and was able to make the social and economic adjustments necessary to feed its own people. India, by contrast, has continued to depend on massive external assistance, a practice that has not only perpetuated its problems, but has compounded them as well.

---

[36] Jack Shepherd, "When Foreign Aid Fails," *The Atlantic Monthly*, April 1985, p. 41.

[37] See Garrett Hardin, "Carrying Capacity as an Ethical Capacity," in George Lucas, Jr., and Thomas Ogletree, eds., *Lifeboat Ethics* (New York: Harper and Row, 1976), pp. 41–43.

In summary, the U.S. government bears a moral responsibility to reduce Third World poverty. I have suggested that the U.S. government should provide additional short-term relief to those people suffering from famine and malnutrition. In the short run this will involve direct aid to those in need. To the extent possible, famine relief should be channeled directly to people in need, avoiding reliance on host governments to distribute aid. But the major challenge is to devise a long-term international economic strategy of job creation. Since there can be no improvement in living conditions in the Third World without an expansion of employment opportunities, the chief aim of any long-term economic assistance strategy must be the promotion of labor-intensive growth. This can be most effectively done when the United States seeks to promote those values, aspirations, practices, and political and economic institutions that have facilitated job creation in the West.

7

THE CHURCH AND FOREIGN POLICY

"It isn't the function of churches to solve problems of diplomacy."

Herbert Butterfield[1]

"The church cannot share the temporal power of the state without being the object of a portion of that animosity which the latter excites."

Alexis de Tocqueville[2]

In May 1984 the general conference of the United Methodist church adopted a resolution calling on people to abolish the "tools of war." The resolution said:

> The vast stockpiles of nuclear bombs and conventional weapons, and the resources being used for arms must be diverted to programs designed to affirm life rather than destroy it. Serious consideration should be given by nations to unilateral initiatives which might stimulate the reaching of international agreement. Governments must renounce use of these particularly inhumane weapons as part of the national policy.[3]

---

[1] Quoted in Kenneth Thompson, *Morality and Foreign Policy* (Baton Rouge: Louisiana State University, 1980), p. 147.

[2] Alexis de Tocqueville, *Democracy in America*, trans. Henry Reeve (New York: Appleton, 1904), 1:334.

[3] United Methodist Church, "Resolution on Disarmament," adopted by the general conference of the United Methodist church, May 1984.

In June 1984 the general board of the American Baptist church, on the recommendation of the denomination's international ministries board, adopted a resolution on Central America, urging the U.S. government to accept more refugees from Central America and to "lend its strength and prestige to the rejection of a military approach, in favor of a policy of negotiation and empowerment. . . ."[4]

During the same month the 196th general assembly of the Presbyterian church adopted numerous foreign policy resolutions, the most extensive one dealing with Central America. The resolution, approved without debate, stated in part:

> Present U.S. policy in Central America continues to be focused on the perceived threat of an expanding Soviet influence in the region, with the virtual neglect of those fundamental economic and social-political reforms that are preconditions to a peaceful resolution of the civil war that for several decades has torn apart the region.[5]

The resolution also urged the United States to stop intervening in Nicaragua, to bring pressure to bear on the government of El Salvador in order to prosecute and punish death squads, and to halt any aid to the government of El Salvador until a negotiated peace settlement had been reached.

A year later the Presbyterian general assembly adopted a similar resolution condemning U.S. foreign policy and rejecting the administration's claim that Nicaragua constituted a threat to the national security and foreign policy of the United States. The resolution specifically opposed the U.S. trade embargo instituted against Nicaragua in mid 1985, and called on President Reagan to repeal the executive order establishing this policy. In addition, the resolution encouraged the "sanctuary" movement by commending congregations who had declared themselves as sanctuary communities and calling on other churches to do so. The general assembly also called on each presbytery to establish a task force to undergird the "ministry of sanctuary" and committed a hundred thousand dollars for the legal defense of those accused of violating U.S. law.[6]

---

[4] American Baptist Church, "Resolution on Central America," June 1984.
[5] United Presbyterian Church, "General Assembly Resolution on Central America," *Church & Society*, July–Aug. 1984, p. 50.
[6] United Presbyterian Church, "General Assembly Resolution on Central America," *Church & Society*, July–Aug. 1985, pp. 12–16.

Are church resolutions such as these beneficial to the body politic and to the church? Is the official involvement of the church in the major public policy debates conducive to a moral foreign policy? Do the views, opinions, and resolutions articulated by official organs of religious bodies contribute to peace and justice in the world? It is important to stress that the issue is not whether the church should be involved in the affairs of state and of the world. I argued earlier that Christians have a responsibility to serve as redemptive agents in reforming the corrupt and unjust structures of political regimes and of international organizations. The issue is not whether Christians should be involved in world affairs and in influencing U.S. foreign policy, but how this task should be undertaken.

The aim of this chapter is to examine the legitimate role of the church in promoting a moral foreign policy. I shall begin by identifying the mission of the church and how that mission relates to the political affairs of state, especially to the international responsibilities of government. I shall then, by examining three contemporary foreign policy concerns of the United States, explore how the church can carry out its redemptive witness in the arena of foreign affairs. Finally, I shall look at how biblical principles can be related to the challenges of diplomacy. Since the bishops' pastoral letter on nuclear strategy is an excellent example of how the Christian faith can inform the moral debate on key foreign affairs issues, I shall examine some of the positive features of that document.

A central argument of this chapter is that much of the foreign policy activity of churches, especially mainline Protestant churches, has been misguided, politically ineffective, and, more importantly, counterproductive to the mission of the church. The churches have not only failed to contribute to the moral debates on contemporary U.S. foreign policies, but have, through overpoliticization, damaged the moral authority of the church itself. If the church is to be the church, it will have to undertake its task of political evangelism with extreme care. This chapter seeks to illuminate how the church can best carry out its redemptive mission in foreign affairs.

THE MISSION OF THE CHURCH

If we are to identify the proper role of the church in the world, it is important to define what we mean by the church. Peter Hinchliff, following Augustine, has suggested that the church can be defined both as an ideal and temporal community. As an ideal, the church represents the body of Christ, or to use Hinchliff's definition, "Christ in his corporate and representational aspects."[7] As a real institution, the church represents those believers professing a commitment to Jesus Christ and seeking to live in fellowship with him through a particular community—whether a local congregation or a religious denomination. Our concern here is not with the ideal church—that is, the body of Christ on earth—but with the temporal church, especially the denominational structures through which much of the politicized activity of Christians has taken place in the United States in recent years.

Four Church Tasks

David McKenna has noted that a biblical church has four responsibilities: prayer, preaching, teaching, and fellowship.[8] While the teaching responsibility is most directly concerned with the church's redemptive witness in public affairs, all four tasks are essential in the political evangelism of the church. In terms of the first task, Christians have a responsibility to pray for those in political authority and for divine direction in the making and implementation of public policies. They also need to pray for guidance in fulfilling their political obligations as citizens.

The church's preaching priority also has implications for public affairs. The task of preaching involves the proclamation of human sinfulness and the call to repentance. Through preaching the church proclaims the divine judgment and redemption, calling peoples and nations to repentance and to a new life. Because of the universality and totality of sin, all peoples, institutions, and nations are unable to live up to the norms of the kingdom of God. The prophetic task of the church is to proclaim the transcendent norms of justice and

---

[7] Peter Hinchliff, *Holiness and Politics* (Grand Rapids: Eerdmans, 1982), p. 121.

[8] David L. McKenna, "A Political Strategy for the Local Church," *Christianity Today*, April 19, 1985, pp. 20–21.

righteousness and to point out the failure of human beings to live in accord with God's revelation and to call people to repentance. Because nations are especially prone to egotism and self-righteousness, the church has a special responsibility to bring divine standards to bear on the institutions and decisions of public officials.

If preaching is to be authentic, the church must not become identified with a political leader, party, or nation. A church will lose credibility and prophetic authority if it becomes associated with a particular political organization, movement, or state. When Constantine made Christianity the official religion of the Roman Empire, for example, the church lost much of its prophetic power. More recently, the close identification of the Nicaraguan "popular" church with the ruling Sandinistas has resulted in a decline in the church's credibility and moral authority. If the church is to maintain a credible preaching ministry, it must remain above the political and temporal concerns of governments.

The church's third task, teaching, is undoubtedly the most important in public affairs. As a teacher in foreign affairs, the church first must help identify the fundamental moral interests of the nation and, second, provide moral and biblical guidance on public policy debates. Since public officials are often guided by immediate, tangible national interests, the church can help identify the long-term moral interests of a nation. All nations, but especially dominant world powers, have been guided historically by the maximization of political power. While the security of a state is a legitimate concern of people, the church must prod the consciences of citizens by clarifying and articulating the moral basis of the nation's fundamental interests. In chapter 1, I argued that the task of morality in foreign affairs was primarily to illuminate, guide, modify, and refine the conception of the national interest. Similarly, the church must help define the legitimate, long-term international goals of a nation.

The second teaching responsibility of the church is to help frame the foreign policy debates by illuminating relevant biblical principles and major moral assumptions. In the latter part of this chapter I explore how this difficult and complex task of integrating moral principles into the public policy debate can be carried out. What is important to recognize at this point is that the church's competency is not in foreign affairs but in moral and biblical analysis. Its contribution in teaching must necessarily focus on the application of spiritual and moral norms to the conduct of foreign affairs. The church must do what it does best—bring a Christian world view to bear on public policy formation—and avoid doing what it does not do well—namely, devising specific foreign policies in response to contemporary world problems. The first is the responsibility of the church leaders; the second is the task of government officials.

The fourth task of the church is fellowship. The church must demonstrate its faith by modeling the moral virtues that it seeks to promote in the field of public affairs—unity, charity, universality of love, forgiveness, and the sharing of material goods with those in need. If the church is to maintain a credible public witness, it must itself be perceived as a just community.

The mission of the church is not to be a major contestant in the public policy debates or to advise government officials on how to conduct foreign policy, but to help establish the moral framework in which public policy deliberations are carried out and to articulate relevant biblical principles that relate to specific public policy problems. The church has a responsibility to contribute to the foreign policy debates in the United States and to the larger international issues of world justice and peace. Its responsibility is not to give specific public policy advice or to devise concrete institutional proposals, but to articulate and apply biblical and moral principles to the problems of international affairs.

THE LIMITED ROLE OF DENOMINATIONAL RESOLUTIONS

Churches and denominational organizations are often tempted to offer specific public policy advice. Such advice is commonly given in the form of official resolutions or council recommendations. The major Protestant denominations regularly issue pronouncements on a wide variety of foreign policy issues. In recent years the most common pronouncements have been on the arms race, nuclear weapons, and U.S. foreign policy toward Central America. Resolutions, however, are of dubious political consequence and raise significant questions about their moral legitimacy.

There are several problems with denominational resolutions. First, they tend to be too simplistic. Public policy by its very nature does not lend itself to simple moral verdicts. There are no simple solutions to complex problems. Indeed, the offering of a simple solution can only damage the credibility of the organization espousing simplistic recommendations. Second, church resolutions are seldom based on careful biblical or moral analysis. The reason for this is that denominational resolutions are not designed as teaching documents, but as instruments of public advocacy. Their aim is not to inform, but to inspire and mobilize public support and especially to influence the behavior of public officials. In their eagerness to address a vast array of public policy issues, churches seldom take the time to examine foreign policy problems dispassionately and bring biblical principles to bear on problems. Their goal is to offer a policy verdict.

Third, denominational resolutions are seldom representative of the organizations on whose behalf they allegedly speak. There are two reasons for this. First, the leadership of churches has historically been much more liberal politically than the rank and file. One survey of U.S. seminary faculty suggests, for example, that whereas 47 percent of the general public considers itself conservative, only 27 percent of the professors do. Conversely, whereas 21 percent of the general public identifies itself with a liberal political ideology, 50 percent of theology faculty do.[9] The reason for the disparity in views is largely ideological: seminary professors, like other religious elites, tend to be idealistic about world affairs, supportive of international organizations, and more critical of U.S. political and economic institutions and military policies than the general public is. Some of the findings of this survey show that: (1) 70 percent believed that the United States treats the people of the Third World unfairly, (2) 70 percent believed that U.S.-based multinational corporations hurt the poor nations in the Third World, (3) 50 percent believed that repressive regimes aligned with the United States were a greater problem than communist expansion, (4) only 57 percent thought that the United States was a force for good in the world, and (5) 74 percent

---

[9]"Theology Faculty: How They Compare," *This World*, Summer 1982, p. 68.

believed that military expenditures were too high.[10] Since views such as these are not the dominant ones of the church laity, the expression of political views by religious elites will seldom reflect the concerns and views of the membership. A further reason why resolutions are seldom representative is that the church, like other large organizations, is dominated by special interests. As an organization increases in size, it tends to delegate its decision making to administrative heads. This pattern, called "the iron law of oligarchy" by social scientists, is especially evident in political organizations, although church organizations are not immune from this tendency. The result is that the leadership of religious denominations is often out of touch with the rank and file, especially in the larger mainline denominations. Thus when the staffs of religious organizations prepare resolutions and proposals, they often reflect the interests and values of professionals, not the members they represent and on whose behalf they work.

A fourth limitation of denominational resolutions is that they can be divisive. Politics is an arena of much conflict and dispute. When churches take specific positions on complex issues in domestic and foreign affairs, they run the risk of creating bitter conflict within the body of Christ. The church needs to emphasize unity in essentials and diversity in unessentials. When preachers use the pulpit to set forth specific positions on world affairs, they unnecessarily run the risk of losing moral authority and fostering division within the church. To be sure, issues occasionally arise on which the church needs to take a stand, but most foreign policy debates are less decisive than the Jewish holocaust, apartheid, or the Cambodian genocide.

If church resolutions are divisive and even counterproductive, why are they so popular? One possible explanation is that the adoption of resolutions provides churches with the illusion that they are carrying out their mandate of redemptive witness in society. Resolutions do, of course, have the advantage of giving simple, clear signals, but there is little evidence to suggest that simplistic recommendations from religious bodies guide or influence public officials in their deliberations. Indeed, denominational resolutions de-

---

[10] "The Survey: Questions and Responses," *This World*, Summer 1982, pp. 48–49.

tract from the moral authority of the church. When religious bodies offer specific policy recommendations, they must compete with a multitude of views from countless interest groups and lobbies. More importantly, the church's advocacy of specific public policies not only weakens the authority of the church, but runs the risk that its views will be treated as those of a lobby. To the extent that this becomes the case, the church will lose credibility to speak prophetically—that is, to bring moral judgment to bear on the conduct of U.S. diplomacy. The church cannot be both an effective lobby and a moral judge. When the church becomes identified with a specific political agenda or organization, it ceases to have the necessary moral authority required for prophetic judgment.

It is important to remember that in a representative system like the United States, public opinion is the foundation of public policy, and that the decisions and policies of government are, as a general rule, a direct expression of the dominant values of society. The formation of public opinion can be achieved in a variety of ways, not only through specific policy proposals. An important element in public opinion is its moral perspectives and normative orientations. Cultivating a moral ethos is indispensable in a democracy, and the institution best equipped to do this is, of course, the church. Many churches, for example, tried to influence public opinion on U.S. foreign policy toward Central America in the early 1980s by advocating specific policies. It is arguable that the advocacy of specific policies can influence public opinion more than a vigorous campaign to illuminate the importance of moral principles, such as nonviolence, human dignity, political and religious liberty, and equality. Cultivating a moral ethos may not provide denominations with a direct voice in the deliberations of government, but it will provide moral perspective on issues that can illuminate and inspire greater public justice.

THE CHURCH AND PUBLIC POLICY

But what does it mean for the church to faithfully preach and teach redemption in the context of foreign affairs? What does the gospel have to do with Central America, the protection of liberty in Eastern Europe, and the feeding of the poor in Central Africa? The business of the church is not to make foreign policy. The church does not have competency in Latin American politics, nuclear peacekeeping, international trade, or immigration policy. Ecclesiastical officials have limited understanding of the direct, indirect, and unintended consequences of public policy. The competence of church officials lies not in the social sciences, but in biblical and moral discernment. The job of making foreign policy is entrusted to elected and appointed government officials. However tempting it may be to offer policy recommendations on the difficult problems of world politics, religious organizations would be well advised to refrain from offering specific foreign policy advice. If the church is to be effective in public affairs, it must do what it has been called to do and what it does best—namely, to be the salt and light of the world—and to avoid doing that which it does not do well—namely, making foreign policy.

In the first chapter I stressed that the function of morality in foreign affairs was not to offer specific verdicts on complex foreign policy issues, but to bring moral norms to bear on the development and implementation of foreign policy. The task of the church is to bear witness to the moral norms of peace, freedom, justice, and human dignity. Its function is to seek to protect the weak and the oppressed and to promote peace among nations. Since the church does not have competence in public policy, it should not, for example, seek to offer specific recommendations on how the United States should promote peace between NATO and Warsaw Pact nations or advance human rights in nations ruled by military dictatorships. The church has the right and responsibility to prod the conscience of the nation and to promote peace, freedom, and justice among states, but it does not have the competence or authority to tell the president or secretary of state what to do about a particular issue. When a church organization declares, as the Presbyterian church (U.S.A.) has done through several denominational resolutions, that the U.S. government should not give economic assistance to El Salvador, it has exceeded its legitimate sphere of competence.

In *Who Speaks for the Church?*, a critique of the politics of the World Council of Churches, Paul Ramsey calls attention to the limited but vital role of the Christian faith in the making of public policy:

Christian political ethics cannot say what should or must be done but only what may be done. In politics the church is only a theoretician. The religious communities as such should be concerned with perspectives upon politics, with political doctrines, with the direction and structures of common life, not with specific directives. They should seek to clarify and keep wide open the legitimate options for choice, and thus nurture the moral and political ethics of the nation. Their task is not the determination of policy.[11]

To be sure, Christian citizens, including ecclesiastical representatives, have a responsibility to participate in the foreign policy debates, but such participation is undertaken as citizens, not as official representatives of a church denomination.

I will now briefly examine three contemporary foreign affairs issues in order to illustrate how the church can illuminate and apply basic principles to concrete international problems. The three issues I shall discuss are apartheid in South Africa, the presidential visit to Bitburg, and social revolution in Central America. The aim here is to briefly sketch some implications of the church's redemptive witness in each policy arena.

South Africa

The basic foreign policy problem posed by South Africa is the government's officially sanctioned practice of racial discrimination. South Africa, a country of some 30 million people, is comprised of approximately 22 million blacks, 4.7 million whites, 2.7 million coloreds, and 800,000 Indians. Despite their minority status, whites have historically controlled political power in South Africa. Prior to 1948 the government was in the hands of British whites. Since then government has been controlled by the Afriraners—a deeply religious people of largely Dutch descent who comprise about 60 percent of the white population. While racial discrimination was practiced by English-speaking whites, the Afriraner government has significantly increased and institutionalized discrimination.

The basis of ethnic discrimination in South Africa is the

---

[11]Paul Ramsey, *Who Speaks for the Church?* (Nashville: Abingdon, 1967), p. 152.

policy of apartheid (separate development). Although the government of South Africa has passed more than 350 laws promoting ethnic separation, the chief legislative acts institutionalizing apartheid are the Group Areas Act of 1950, which designates the territories in which blacks may live, and the Bantu Self Government Act of 1959, which sets up self-government in tribal homelands. The Bantustan Act says that the blacks are to be resettled into some ten "homelands," each of which is to become a self-governing territory and eventually an independent state. Four of these homelands have already become self-governing entities, but no country except South Africa has recognized their independence. Since the "homelands" act became effective, more than 3.5 million blacks have been uprooted and forced to move to one of the black territories.

Officially, the reason for apartheid is to protect ethnic and cultural diversity. In practice, the policy of apartheid has provided the means by which the white minority has protected its political and economic power and perpetuated its domination of blacks. The plan to establish "homelands" may have been adopted, as officials of the South African government proclaim, as a means to protect the ethnic and cultural diversity of the peoples in that land. But the injustice and discrimination of the apartheid system also lead inescapably to the conclusion that the system of "separate development" has been imposed by the whites as a means of preserving political and economic privileges. How else can one explain the fact that whites, who comprise only 17 percent of the population, are allocated 87 percent of the land? How else can one explain the failure of whites to allow blacks some representation in national politics?

Apartheid is not working, and the reason it is not working is because the industrialization of South Africa, which depends on black labor, has impeded resettlement. Rather than encouraging migration into the "homelands," the economic expansion of South Africa has increased the movement of the blacks into the urban areas where they can find jobs. As a result, during the past twenty years, black "townships" have been created in which blacks can live close to white cities. Soweto, the largest and best known of these, has nearly two million blacks living outside of Johannesburg. The government of South Africa has, of course, tried to control expansion of these townships and has developed an extensive system of "pass laws"—rules that regulate the movement of blacks into urban areas. In order to limit the number of blacks in urban areas, the government has tended to issue permits only to men, thus forcing families to live far away in one of the designated "homelands." But the effort to use law to regulate the movement of blacks has been largely ineffective. In Durban, for example, there are more than a million blacks living in townships, yet only about fifty thousand have legal permits to live in the area.[12]

Apartheid is an affront to human dignity. It is inconsistent with the biblical norms of justice because people are treated unequally under the law.[13] The Scriptures teach the infinite and inherent worth of each human being, regardless of race, social class, or sex. A regime based on the inequality of human persons is clearly inconsistent with biblical teachings. The moral problem with the South African regime is that it is a democracy for whites but a quasi-totalitarian system for blacks. Whites have their own government, but blacks can participate in politics only in the affairs of the regional territories.[14]

What is the church's role in bringing about reform in South Africa? I believe the church's mission is limited primarily to proclaiming the evil of apartheid. The task of the church is not to define how the U.S. government should contribute to the devolution of political power to the blacks, but to condemn the apartheid policy itself. Its job is not to devise foreign policy for the Department of State, but to bear witness to the Scriptures by judging the moral legitimacy of the South African regime.

---

[12]Joseph Lelyveld, "For Pretoria, Laws Are Basic to Keeping Blacks in Check," *New York Times*, Oct. 10, 1983, p. 4.

[13]This point was well made by a resolution adopted in June 1985 by the United Presbyterian church general assembly. The resolution stated that "apartheid (Separate Development) is a sin, and that the moral and theological justification of it is a travesty of the Gospel, and in its persistent disobedience to the Word of God, a theological heresy" ("Divestment for South Africa: An Investment in Hope," *Church & Society*, July–Aug. 1985, p. 21).

[14]The increasing international pressure on South Africa led Prime Minister Botha to modify the constitutional system of the state. In 1983 a new constitutional system was approved, permitting political participation of coloreds and Indians in national affairs. The new system expanded the parliament to include two additional chambers—one for Indians and one for coloreds. Since whites maintain complete control of the parliament, the reforms have been, at best, cosmetic.

The church's task, then, is not to devise a system of reform, but to bring judgment to bear on the repugnant and unjust practice of racial discrimination. There is ample evidence that many blacks in South Africa have benefited from South Africa's economic growth of the past twenty years. The standard of living of most South African blacks is substantially higher than that in neighboring African countries, but the improvement in living standards does not and cannot justify a political system that excludes some peoples from political participation and treats them unequally before the law. Racial discrimination makes apartheid a wholly unacceptable moral system.

Since the church is not responsible for devising public policies, how the U.S. government seeks to bring about reform in a foreign state is a matter on which well-informed diplomats will disagree. It is therefore unwise for churches to become involved in the intricacies of public policy making, lest their participation result in a decline in their moral authority. That apartheid is morally repugnant cannot be denied; what is less clear is how the U.S. government should contribute to the promotion of human dignity in South Africa. Many religious denominations have, for example, advocated specific policies, including the imposition of economic sanctions and disinvestment. Whether or not such policies will in fact promote human dignity is open to doubt. One of the most articulate South African critics, Alan Paton, writes critically about disinvestment:

> I have a word to say to those Americans who think they can hasten the "day of liberation" by damaging the South African, as for example, by disinvestment. I do not think that damaging our economy will help us to do better. It will do material harm to many black people. Americans ought to be told that they are going to bring hunger and suffering to many black people. One often hears black South Africans cry: "We don't mind suffering. We are used to it." But this cry usually comes from those articulate blacks who will suffer least. I, as a Christian, will have nothing to do with disinvestment. To believe that disinvestment will bring our Government "to its knees" is to believe nonsense.[15]

---

[15] Alan Paton, "South Africa Is in a Mess," *New York Times,* April 3, 1985, p. 27.

Churches concerned with South African political affairs would be well advised to focus on the injustice of apartheid and avoid the specifics of reform. The church should continue to bring its moral authority to bear on the conditions of that nation, challenging governments and international organizations to promote policies that protect individual rights and human dignity. Since the church knows little about diplomacy and the processes of political development, it should avoid giving specific advice on how the United States should undertake its relations with a nation whose basic institutional practices are an affront to American democratic values.

Bitburg

The presidential visit to Bitburg, West Germany, in May 1985 also provides another moral case in foreign affairs. Shortly after President Reagan announced that he would be visiting the military cemetery at Bitburg, an intense debate arose about the appropriateness of such a visit after it was discovered that former SS troops were buried there. The original aim for visiting a World War II German–American cemetery was to commemorate the ending of the war and the establishment of peaceful U.S.–German relations during the subsequent forty years. Government officials of both the United States and West Germany believed that, in the light of strong, consistent, and cordial relations between the two nations, such a visit could symbolize the significant evolution in European international relations since 1945.

After Bitburg had been selected as a site for a joint commemorative visit by President Reagan and Chancellor Helmut Kohl, officials discovered that forty-eight SS troops were buried at the cemetery. This discovery precipitated an intense public debate about whether or not President Reagan should visit Bitburg. Many Americans, but especially Jews, felt that such a visit would represent a callous disregard for the pain and suffering endured by the Jewish people during the Second World War.

With the exception of the Jewish community, religious groups and churches were virtually silent on the Bitburg debate. Through its silence, the church forfeited an opportunity to bring moral principles to bear on an important foreign policy problem. The church was correct in not giving President Reagan advice on whether or not to visit Bitburg, but the church could have and should have proclaimed the biblical teachings relevant to this issue. At a minimum, the church could have reminded government officials and the public of the reality of sin, manifest throughout all history but especially in the holocaust tragedy, while also proclaiming the message of repentance, renewal, and forgiveness. The gospel is the "good news" that sin can be overcome through the reconciling work of Christ. Despite the evil of the past, the Christian message is one of hope to those who repent.

To President Reagan's credit, he called attention to both biblical themes in his Bitburg visit by emphasizing sin and forgiveness, judgment and reconciliation, tragedy and promise. At the Bitburg U.S. Air Force Base, after visiting the cemetery, he said:

> The one lesson of World War II, the one lesson of Nazism, is that freedom must always be·stronger than totalitarianism, and that good must always be stronger than evil. The moral measure of our two nations will be found in the resolve we show to preserve liberty, to protect life and to honor and cherish all God's children. That is why the free, democratic Federal Republic of Germany is such a profound and hopeful testament to the human spirit. We cannot undo the crimes and wars of yesterday, nor call the millions back to life. But we can give meaning to the past by learning its lessons and making a better future. We can let our pain drive us to greater efforts to heal humanity's suffering. . . . on this 40th anniversary of World War II, we mark the day when the hate, the evil and the obscenities ended, and we commemorate the rekindling of the democratic spirit in Germany.[16]

Central America

Unlike the Bitburg conflict, the problems of Central America have been one of the dominant foreign policy concerns of the churches in the 1980s. The major foreign policy problem is how the United States should respond to the increasing turmoil in the region but especially in El Salvador and Nicaragua.

The problem posed by Nicaragua is the increasingly radical revolutionary character of the government. The

---

[16]Ronald Reagan, "Speech at U.S. Air Base, Bitburg," *New York Times*, May 6, 1985, p. 8.

source of the turmoil is the Sandinista leadership, which has attempted to transform Nicaragua into a quasi-totalitarian communist society. Since assuming power in 1979, the Sandinistas have, with Cuban and Eastern-bloc nations' assistance, sought to consolidate power and to establish a Leninist organizational network for the regulation of society. The regime has all but eliminated free press, significantly curtailed the role of unions, and limited the role of the church. By 1980 the Sandinistas had alienated a significant portion of Nicaraguan society, and by 1982 a counterrevolutionary force (Contra) comprised of alienated Sandinistas and former members of the Somoza national guard had begun to challenge the Sandinista militia and military forces. Meanwhile relations with the United States had become increasingly strained, especially after the United States began to assist the Contras.

The situation in El Salvador differs from Nicaragua in that there has been insurgency but no revolution. During the past two decades the country has experienced substantial modernization; but the political, economic, and social institutions of society have been slow to adapt to the increasing demands of the poor people. Wealth and power were historically controlled by a small landed elite, and efforts to transform the social and economic structures of society have been painfully slow. In the early 1980s leftist guerrillas, with significant external assistance, were able to expand their influence considerably; and by 1982 they controlled a large portion of the countryside. The guerrillas were unsuccessful in their effort to bring down the government, however, and by 1985 they had lost a significant portion of the influence they had enjoyed in the early 1980s. The reason for their military failure was in large part due to the substantial economic and military assistance of the United States, the ratification of a new constitution, the transition to full democracy in 1984, and the election of Jose Napoleon Duarte, the popular Christian Democratic party leader.

Protestant denominations have been highly critical of U.S. foreign policies toward both these countries and have issued countless statements and resolutions in an attempt to influence congressional deliberations. In the main, the churches have defined the regional tensions chiefly in social and economic terms and have viewed the United States as a hindrance to indigenous political and social development. As a result, the churches have opposed most U.S. foreign policies that have sought to influence the evolution of events in the region. Some of the most common positions advocated by churches include: (1) support for a negotiated political settlement of the insurgency in El Salvador, (2) cessation of U.S. assistance to the Contras in Nicaragua, (3) affirmation of the right of national self-determination, and (4) opposition to economic and military aid to the government of El Salvador.

In assessing the church's involvement in the Central America debate, it is important to determine whether the church has illuminated key biblical and moral principles relative to the regional tensions and whether it has applied them dispassionately. I believe that the church's record has been only partially successful in the first task and largely ineffective in the second.

Churches have legitimately affirmed the principle of peace, and they have also been correct in affirming human life, but the articulation of biblical justice has been incomplete, for the churches have focused almost exclusively on economic welfare and have neglected political freedom. The failure to emphasize political and religious freedom is especially regrettable, for the expanding sphere of the state has historically been one of the most destructive forces to the church. However, the chief shortcoming of the churches' Central American foreign policy has been the overemphasis on specific public policy recommendations and the failure to illuminate the moral dimensions of the public policy debate.

The churches' involvement in Central American foreign affairs has also led to inconsistent applications. For example, the churches have proposed political negotiation in El Salvador but not in Nicaragua. They have also opposed the counterrevolutionary forces in Nicaragua but not the revolutionary guerrillas in El Salvador. They have affirmed the principle of life in Nicaragua but not in El Salvador. The reason for these different applications is not biblical exegesis or moral analysis but political ideology. Because of their liberal ideological sympathies, ecclesiastical officials have underestimated the conflict between totalitarianism and democracy and the influence of Soviet-bloc states in Nicaragua. For example, they have specifically discounted the increasing militarism in Nicaragua, underestimated the radical character of the guerrillas in El Salvador, and discounted the Cuban and Eastern European military and political influence in the evolution of the Sandinista regime. Moreover, whereas the secular media has provided substantial evidence of the increasing politicization of society and the threats to pluralism, the churches have been virtually silent about these developments, especially the threat they pose to the independence and vitality of the church.[17]

The churches' involvement in the Central American dilemma raises numerous questions and concerns. It is difficult, for example, to understand on what basis the religious organizations have continued their support of the Sandinistas while opposing the emerging democratic forces and institutions of El Salvador. Moreover, it is even more difficult to understand why so many Protestant churches have opposed U.S. assistance to El Salvador, especially in the light of the continuing threat posed by leftist guerrillas receiving external support. But the problems are not solely with the substantive views espoused by the churches. There is, however, a more serious issue. This involves the loss of the church's moral authority from the politicization and overinvolvement in the specifics of the public policy debates. By focusing on concrete diplomatic issues, the church has neglected to do that which it does best—to illuminate and apply biblical norms of justice to the realities of Central America in a general and dispassionate manner. Rather than bringing moral judgment and direction to the issues, the church has itself become a participant in the public policy debate. As a result, the church has failed to provide the guidance and direction which it otherwise may have given.

THE INTEGRATION OF FAITH AND POLICY

Successfully integrating the Christian faith and foreign policy is not easy. The development of public policy from a Christian perspective is difficult because it requires competence in biblical and moral analysis and in foreign affairs. A sound and careful integration of faith and public policy will require at least four distinct steps or stages. The first involves the clarification and illumination of relevant biblical princi-

---

[17] For an excellent examination of the decline of pluralism in Nicaragua see Stephen Kinzer, "Nicaragua: The Beleaguered Revolution," *The New York Times Magazine*, Aug. 28, 1983; and Shirley Christian, *Nicaragua: Revolution in the Family* (New York: Random House, 1985).

ples. The second involves the development of knowledge about the particular problem or issue. The challenge here is to get the facts and become thoroughly familiar with the essential elements of the problem, including historical, social, political, and economic factors. The third stage involves the development and application of a relevant political theory which best affirms human dignity and international peace and justice. The fourth and final stage involves the application of moral and biblical principles to the problem at hand in the light of the political theory illuminated in the third stage. The goal in this stage is to illuminate the key elements of the problem in the light of the moral and political analysis and to identify possible alternative solutions.

The development of competence in biblical and political analysis cannot be overemphasized. When Christians speak in the name of the Lord, they need spiritual and moral competency on the one hand and sound political knowledge on the other. Only after proceeding carefully through the first three stages can Christians effectively integrate faith and foreign policy. As a teacher, the church can of course illuminate biblical and moral principles and challenge its members to become more informed about the concrete foreign policy issues of the government. Perhaps the most difficult stage is the third—the development of a political theory that builds on the values and norms of the first two. It is important in this stage to identify the nature and character of the political institutions and practices necessary for the implementation of desired goals.

It is beyond the scope of this chapter to explore which principles, practices, and institutions are most consistent with Christian norms. Such a task is exceptionally difficult because Christians have historically defined justice and human dignity in a variety of ways and also because they have interpreted the relationship of faith to politics differently. The result is that there is no domestic or international political theory which is universally accepted in the church. Nonetheless, there is substantial agreement among Christians about the desirability for a regime based on values such as order, equality, participation, and freedom. Such a government, of necessity, must be a limited, participatory regime that protects peoples' rights through due process of law. But an effective political theory must go beyond the articulation of general goals such as these. It must explain which institutions and political rules and practices are most likely to protect and promote social justice and political liberty. What is needed, then, is a body of theory identifying and explaining the role of legal and constitutional instruments as well as social practices necessary in securing limited government and promoting economic well-being.[18]

If church organizations active in foreign policy were to approach their task of political evangelism with greater care and seek to apply the four-stage model outlined above, their political and moral influence would increase immeasurably. To be sure, churches would undoubtedly issue fewer resolutions and pronouncements, but their credibility as moral teachers would undoubtedly improve. A more discriminating political involvement of churches would have one other desirable outcome: it would decrease the misuse and overuse of the Scriptures for political ends. It is important to stress again that the Bible does not give specific public policy guidance. Regrettably, religious organizations have commonly sought to defend liberal or conservative public policy positions with biblical citations. It is important to remember that the Bible is not a foreign policy manual, but is God's revelation to all people. As a witness of God's activity and presence, the Bible issues, as Jeffrey Siker notes, "a call to repentance, a call to commitment and a call to be in the world but not of it."[19]

The Bishops' Pastoral Letter on Nuclear Weapons

During the late 1970s and early 1980s, the American public became increasingly concerned with the evolution of nuclear strategy, and many religious groups and churches became deeply involved in the public debate. Some churches passed resolutions, others prepared study documents, and

---

[18] An illuminating study on the interrelationship of political and economic institutions and political and economic well-being is Michael Novak's theory of democratic capitalism. According to Novak, economic productivity and political liberty are maximized under democratic, constitutional rules, while economic productivity is maximized under conditions of free enterprise. Novak suggests that the democratic political system and the capitalistic economic system are not only complementary but necessary for each system's maximum effectiveness. For a full exploration of Novak's theory, see *The Spirit of Democratic Capitalism* (New York: Simon and Schuster, 1982).

[19] Jeffrey S. Siker, "The Bible and Public Policy," *The Christian Century*, Feb. 19, 1986, p. 172.

most sought to influence the decision-making process of government through organized lobbying. Most church documents and resolutions were advocacy documents, reflecting little analysis of this complex issue. The principal effort of the U.S. Catholic church to respond to the public debate involved the preparation of a pastoral letter entitled "The Challenge of Peace."[20] Because this study illustrates how a church can competently carry out its public affairs teaching ministry, I want to examine briefly some of the key elements of that document and point out why it stands as one of the most credible contributions of the church to a foreign policy debate.

I have written elsewhere about my dissatisfaction with the arguments made by the pastoral letter.[21] What concerns me here, however, is not the substance of the letter, but the role of that document as a teaching device—as an instrument to inform and apply biblical and moral reasoning to one of the major public policy issues of our time. Judged from that perspective, no church study undertaken in recent years in the United States has applied moral and biblical reasoning to a complex foreign policy problem with greater thoroughness and dispassion.

The bishops' letter is an enormously important document. Its significance derives in part from the timing of its drafting and publication. When the bishops first began to prepare the letter in early 1981, there was a growing popular concern with arms control and nuclear strategy. This interest continued to expand in the subsequent two years during which the letter was under preparation. When the final draft was adopted in May 1983 the general public was eagerly searching for moral guidance from the church.

A second reason for the pastoral letter's significance is that it was prepared with unusual professional care. In writing the letter, the bishops involved some of the most knowledgeable thinkers on ethics, theology, foreign policy, and national security. Moreover, the bishops provided ample opportunity for discussion and debate over the two years during which the letter was being prepared.

A third reason for the importance of the letter lies in the

---

[20] U.S. Catholic Bishops, "The Challenge of Peace: God's Promise and Our Response," The Pastoral Letter on War and Peace, *Origins*, May 19, 1983.

[21] Mark R. Amstutz, "The Challenge of Peace: Did the Bishops Help?" *This World* 11 (Spring/Summer 1985).

letter's integration of biblical and moral reasoning with the realities of nuclear strategy. The bishops recognize that their competence is not in national security affairs. Nonetheless, they seek to interpret the moral and religious wisdom of the Catholic tradition and to apply it to the problems of war and peace. While the bishops' letter offers policy recommendations, the primary aim and contribution of the study is the assessment of nuclear strategy in the light of biblical and moral principles.

The pastoral letter comprises four parts: (1) theological, biblical, and moral perspectives on peacekeeping, including an assessment of the just war tradition; (2) the problem of peacekeeping through nuclear deterrence; (3) proposals and policies for promoting peace in the nuclear age; and (4) a pastoral challenge to the church and selected constituencies. A major strength of the letter is its succinct but careful analysis of biblical and moral principles applicable to the nuclear dilemma and the careful assessment of the problem posed by the evolution of nuclear strategy. The bishops emphasize that their authority does not extend equally to all parts or sections of the letter. They stress that moral principles are to be considered binding while the application of those principles to specific cases are not. The bishops write:

> When making applications of these principles we realize—and we wish readers to recognize that prudential judgments are involved based on specific circumstances which can change or which can be interpreted differently by people of good will. . . . the moral judgments that we make in specific cases, while not binding in conscience, are to be given serious attention and consideration by Catholics as they determine whether their moral judgments are consistent with the Gospel.[22]

The bishops recognize that the application of moral and biblical principles to an emotional and volatile issue such as nuclear strategy has the potential for increasing division within the church. That is why they remind readers that no Christian is allowed to appropriate the church's authority for his opinion. Rather Christians "should always try to enlighten one another through honest discussion, preserving mutual charity and caring above all for the common good."

---

[22]U.S. Catholic Bishops, "The Challenge of Peace," p. 3.

The letter continues, "Not only conviction and commitment are needed in the church, but also civility and charity."[23] The bishops' letter does not include all of the elements of the public policy model outlined above. One important omission is the absence of a theory of peacekeeping in the light of the dominant world confrontation between the East and the West, democracy and communist totalitarianism. The problem of nuclear strategy is presented as a military issue isolated from the international political realities of superpower relationships. There is virtually no reference to the global tensions between the United States and the Soviet Union or to the values and ideologies represented by each state. The problem of nuclear peacekeeping appears, therefore, in total isolation of the search for international justice. This is a grave omission.

Peace among states, however, is not the sole aim guiding Christian foreign policy. If world harmony were the only objective in international politics, the peacekeeping task would be infinitely simpler: the church would recommend the immediate dismantling of all nuclear and conventional armories, leaving the task of justice in the hands of the Almighty. But the quest is not for peace alone, but for a just peace. The task, as George Weigel has noted, is to build "rightly-ordered" political communities that mutually affirm peace, freedom, security and prosperity.[24] Moreover, while peace is a divine gift, it is also the result of human efforts. Christians must therefore pray for justice and peace, but they must also work for peace by thoughtfully developing and supporting policies that encourage a more harmonious, humane, and just world.

The pastoral letter on nuclear peacekeeping is an enormously important document not because of its conclusions, but because of the thoroughness of its analysis of the dilemma of nuclear strategy and the care in illuminating relevant moral and biblical principles. More than one-half of the pastoral letter is devoted to an exposition of biblical perspectives on war and peace and the moral dimensions of nuclear deterrence. By meticulously integrating biblical, moral, and strategic concerns, the bishops performed compe-

---

[23]Ibid.

[24]George Weigel, *Tranquillitas Ordinis: The Present Failure and Future Promise of American Catholic Thought on War and Peace* (New York: Oxford, 1987), pp. 184–90, 356–59.

tently the teaching task to which they are called. While they did not shun specific policy proposals, the major message of the church's letter is that nuclear war is morally unacceptable and that every effort needs to be made to avoid it. By focusing primarily on the biblical and moral dimensions of nuclear peacekeeping, the Catholic church did what it can do best, which is to clarify and illuminate moral principles.

Mainline Protestant churches could contribute much more to the making of foreign policy if they carried out their teaching task more faithfully and more responsibly. But they can do so only if they inform, guide, and challenge Christians on fewer, more foundational, issues in domestic and international politics. The church has a responsibility to assume in foreign affairs. Its role, however, is not to make foreign policy, but to help structure the context in which public policy is debated and to apply moral principles to specific foreign policy problems of our time.

SELECTED ANNOTATED BIBLIOGRAPHY

Beitz, Charles, et al., eds. *International Ethics.* Princeton, N.J.: Princeton University Press, 1985. A collection of influential journal articles dealing with the ethics of war, deterrence, the legitimacy of states, and distributive justice.

Bennett, John C. *Foreign Policy in Christian Perspective.* New York: Charles Scribner's Sons, 1966. While some of the material in this book is dated, the first two and last chapters dealing with Christian ethics and foreign policy and the role of the church in world affairs continue to be relevant.

———, and Seifert, Harvey. *U.S. Foreign Policy and Christian Ethics.* Philadelphia: Westminster Press, 1977. This study updates Bennett's 1966 volume. This study provides a useful introduction to ethical issues in U.S. foreign policy. The analysis of some specific issues, however, is superficial.

Clouse, Robert G., ed. *War: Four Christian Views.* Downers Grove: Intervarsity Press, 1981. The problem of war is examined from four different theological perspectives: nonresistance, Christian pacifism, just war, and crusade or preventive war.

Coll, Alberto R. *The Wisdom of Statecraft: Sir Herbert Butterfield and the Philosophy of International Politics.* Durham: Duke University Press, 1985. A competent and thoughtful analysis and assessment of Butterfield's Christian approach to world politics.

Curry, Dean C., ed. *Evangelicals and the Bishops' Pastoral Letter.* Grand Rapids: Wm. B. Eerdmans Publishing Co., 1984. Twelve evangelical scholars examine various aspects of the Catholic bishops' pastoral letter on nuclear weapons.

Dougherty. James E. *The Bishops and Nuclear Weapons.* Hamden, Conn.: Archon Books, 1984. This is perhaps the most discriminating assessment of the 1983 bishops' pastoral letter on nuclear weapons and peacekeeping.

Fisher, David. *Morality and the Bomb.* New York: St. Martin's Press, 1985. An informed, thoughtful defense of deterrence using just war criteria by a British civil servant involved in national security issues.

Hare, J. E., and Joynt, Carey B. *Ethics and International Affairs.* New York: St. Martin's Press, 1982. Hare, a philosopher, and Joynt, a political scientist, combine their efforts to produce a penetrating philosophical assessment of the problem of ethics and foreign affairs. The book focuses on war, deterrence, arms control, and the legitimacy of the contemporary world order.

Hesburgh, Theodore M., and Halle, Louis J. *Foreign Policy and Morality: Framework for Moral Audit.* New York: Council on Religion and International Affairs, 1979. Hesburgh and Halle present different views of the role of morality in U.S. foreign policy. Five illuminating critiques of the two lectures follow.

Hoffman, Stanley. *Duties Beyond Borders.* Syracuse: Syracuse University Press, 1981. A theoretical and philosophic examination of the limits and possibilities of ethical international relations. Four issues are examined: the use of force, the promotion of human rights, distributive justice, and the nature of world order.

Lefever, Ernest. *Ethics and United States Foreign Policy.* New York: World Publishing Co., 1967. An analysis of the U.S. foreign policy from the perspective of Christian realism. The book has recently been reissued by University Press.

————, ed. *Morality and Foreign Policy.* Washington, D.C.: Ethics and Public Policy Center, 1977. A presentation of Jimmy Carter's famous Notre Dame University speech, "Power for Humane Purposes," followed by the critique of twelve distinguished political commentators. A pointed debate on the role of ethics in diplomacy.

Muravchik, Joshua. *The Uncertain Crusade.* Lanham, Md.: Hamilton Press, 1986. A competent examination and assessment of Jimmy Carter's human rights policy. Part 2 of the study, which addresses the dilemmas of promoting human rights abroad, is especially useful.

Nardin, Terry. *Law, Morality, and the Relations of States.* Princeton: Princeton University Press, 1983. While the bulk of this study concerns the nature and role of international law in the world, the last four chapters focus on the relationship of morality, international law, and world peace.

Norman, Edward. *Christianity and World Order.* Oxford: Oxford University Press, 1979. This short book is based on Norman's B.B.C. Reith Lectures of 1978. Norman provides a trenchant critique of the overpoliticization of the church in world affairs.

Nye, Joseph, Jr. *Nuclear Ethics.* New York: The Free Press, 1986. A readable, introductory moral assessment of nuclear deterrence by a leading political scientist.

Thompson, Kenneth. *Moral Dimensions of American Foreign Policy.* New Brunswick: Transaction Books, 1984. A series of essays, originally published by the Council on Religion and International Affairs, dealing with such topics as intervention, war, deterrence, and foreign aid.

————. *The Moral Issue in Statecraft.* Baton Rouge: Louisiana State University Press, 1966. Thompson, one of the leading Christian realists, argues against universal moralism and defends the prudential application of power in international politics.

———, ed. *Ethics and International Relations*. Ethics and Foreign Policy. Vol. 2. New Brunswick: Transaction Books, 1985. A collection of essays dealing with the relationship of morality and diplomacy. Thompson's essay "Ethics and International Relations: The Problem" and Michael Smith's "Moral Reasoning and Moral Responsibility in International Affairs" are especially illuminating and thoughtful.

Walzer, Michael. *Just and Unjust Wars*. New York: Basic Books, 1977. Walzer argues through historical illustrations that moral standards apply in warfare. This philosophic book is a major contribution to the understanding of ethics and world affairs because it provides a framework for assessing the behavior of states in world politics.

Weigel, George. *Tranquillitas Ordinis*. New York: Oxford University Press, 1987. A thoughtful, comprehensive attack on the political evolution of the American Catholic church in the post-Vatican II era. Weigel argues that American Catholic leaders have abandoned the historical tradition of political realism in favor of current political trends. He calls the church to a more reflective political engagement.